How We Get Things

H○w We

Get Things

A supplement to
Childcraft—The How and Why Library

World Book, Inc.
a Scott Fetzer company
Chicago   London   Sydney   Toronto

Contents

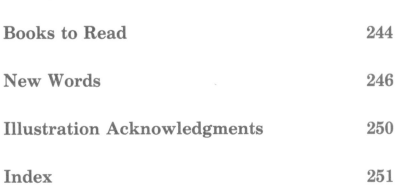

Preface

How was this book made? Where did your pencil come from? How did we get bikes and roller skates? Think of all the things around you. They have a story to tell!

Maybe that story is about how those things are made today. Perhaps the story is about how something, like a bicycle, got to be the way it is today from the way it used to be. Or, maybe the story is about how something else, like a television picture, gets *to* you.

How We Get Things is many stories. Watch for the little bird, called a toucan (TOO kan), to help you through. Try the Fun-to-Do projects, and get to make things yourself. Most of all, enjoy finding out about so many of the things around us—and how we get them.

Hello. I'm a toucan. Watch for me in this book. I help explain words and I give extra facts.

ew, and Slurp

THINGS WE EAT AND DRINK

What is bread made of?

How do the holes get in Swiss cheese?

How do we get the chew in chewing gum?

Where does the fizz in soda pop come from?

New, Improved: Bread!

Maybe you remember the story of Little Red Hen, who couldn't get her lazy friends to help her make bread. Here's a new version. This time, Little Red Hen uses machines to help her make bread. Bread begins as wheat, which is a plant.

The wheat in the field had grown tall and golden. Little Red Hen said, "The wheat is ripe now. Who will help me cut it?"

"Not I," said the duck.

"Not I," said the cat.

"Not I," said the dog.

"Very well," said Little Red Hen. "I
will use a machine called a combine to
cut the wheat. The combine will also
remove the husk, or covering, from the
wheat kernels and pour the grain into
my truck."

Soon, Little Red Hen had a truck
full of wheat grain.

Then she asked, "Now who's ready
to help me grind the wheat into flour?"

"Not I," said the duck.

"Not I," said the cat.

"Not I," said the dog.

"I should have known," replied
Little Red Hen. "Very well. I will take
my wheat to a flour mill."

At the mill, Little Red Hen's wheat flowed into a big grinder. The grain was ground and sifted until it became a fine flour. Machines put the flour into bags and sealed the bags shut.

Little Red Hen left the mill with a truck full of flour bags.

"Who's ready to help me make bread out of my flour?" she asked.

"Not I," said the duck.

"Not I," said the cat.

"Not I," said the dog.

"I just thought I'd ask," said Little Red Hen. "Very well. I will take my flour to a bakery."

Not I!

At the bakery, a machine mixed the flour with water, yeast, salt, and oil. It became a sticky blob of dough. The dough sat in a tank in a warm room until the yeast made the dough rise to double its size.

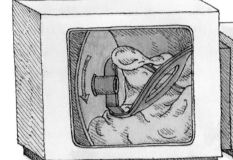

Mixing

Rising

The dough then moved on a belt from one machine to another. The first machine cut the dough into pieces. The next shaped the pieces into loaves. The third dropped the loaves into baking pans.

Cutting

Panning

Shaping

15

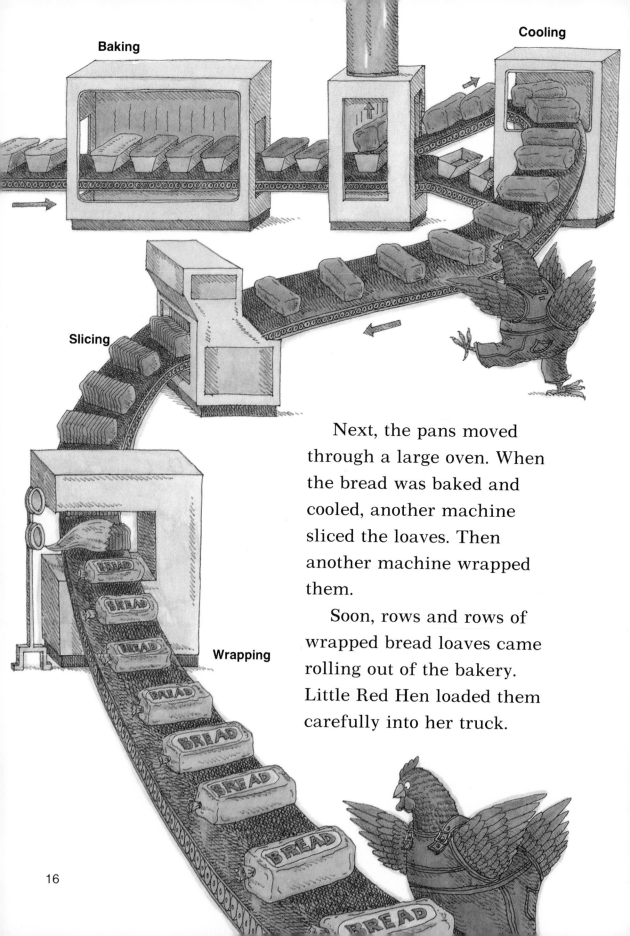

Baking

Cooling

Slicing

Wrapping

Next, the pans moved through a large oven. When the bread was baked and cooled, another machine sliced the loaves. Then another machine wrapped them.

Soon, rows and rows of wrapped bread loaves came rolling out of the bakery. Little Red Hen loaded them carefully into her truck.

"My, my," she exclaimed. "I wonder who will help me eat this tasty fresh bread."

"I will!" said the duck.

"I will!" said the cat.

"I will!" said the dog.

"Not so fast, my friends!" said Little Red Hen. "You did not cut the wheat or grind it into flour. You did not mix the flour into dough or bake the dough into bread. If you want to eat my tasty bread, you will have to buy it."

So the duck, cat, and dog each bought a loaf of bread. And Little Red Hen happily counted her money.

"I don't mind so much that my friends didn't help me make bread," she said to herself. "The combine, the mill, and the bakery made the job much easier anyway."

Make a Little Bread Hen

You Will Need:

6 slices of soft white
   bread
6 teaspoons of white
   glue
½ teaspoon liquid
   detergent
a few drops of red
   food coloring
bowl
spoon
notebook paper
   and pencil
small scissors
wax paper
metal can or small
   rolling pin
toothpick
1 tablespoon glue
1 tablespoon water
paint brush
lacquer

You've just read how Little Red Hen made bread out of wheat. How would you like to make a Little Red Hen out of bread?

1. Take the crusts off the bread. (You can feed them to the birds.)

2. Break the bread into tiny crumbs in the bowl.

3. Add the 6 teaspoons of glue, liquid detergent, and food coloring. Stir.

4. Mix the dough with your hands until it becomes a smooth ball.

5. Put notebook paper over the picture of Little Red Hen shown here. Trace the hen's outline on the paper.

6. Cut out your picture of Little Red Hen.

18

*Don't forget to ask your parents for permission.

7. On the wax paper, roll the dough flat so it is about as thick as one of your fingers.

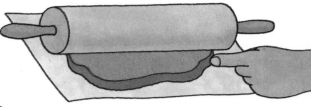

8. Stick your picture of Little Red Hen onto the dough. Using the picture as a guide, cut out a hen from the dough.

9. Use the toothpick to carve Little Red Hen's eye and wing.

10. Mix the tablespoon of glue and water. With the brush, paint this glue mixture on the hen. This will keep the dough from cracking as it dries.

11. Leave your dough hen on the wax paper in a cool, dry place for about 12 hours.

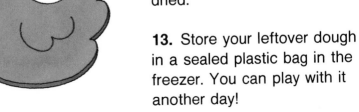

12. If you want your hen to last a long time, ask your mom or dad to help you coat it with lacquer when it is dried.

13. Store your leftover dough in a sealed plastic bag in the freezer. You can play with it another day!

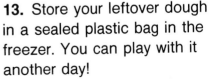

The Great Moo Machine

"How about a glass of magic moo juice, Sis?" Billy offered.

Sarah saw her younger brother holding up a glass of white liquid.

"Magic moo juice?" Sarah said. "Silly Billy, that's just a glass of milk."

"Some people call it milk," said Billy. "I like to think of it as juice from the Great Moo Machine."

"Great Moo Machine?" said Sarah.

"The Great Moo Machine is a wonder!" Billy said. "You pour grass, hay, and water into it. It gives out a great moo. Then out pop cartons of milk and cream and sticks of butter . . . ."

Did You Know?

Pasteurization (pas chuhr uh ZAY shuhn) was named after the French scientist who discovered it, Louis Pasteur. Pasteur found that diseases are spread by germs. So he invented pasteurization, a method of preserving foods by killing off harmful germs that would make people sick. When a food is pasteurized, it is heated to a specific temperature for a certain amount of time. The heat kills off the harmful germs.

"Cows make milk, Billy, not some machine," said Sarah. "I know because my class went to a dairy farm and dairy plant last week. We learned that cows make so much milk, they can feed their young and still have milk left over for us.

"The cows we saw were eating grass and hay and drinking water, but they were also eating soybean meal and corn. The dairy farmer told us that this makes the milk extra good for us.

"When the cows are ready for milking, this is what happens. . . .

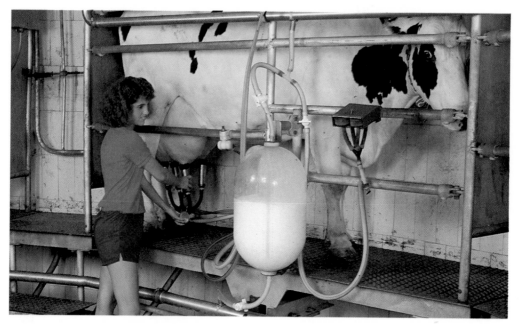

"Machines milk the cow.

"When the milk comes out of the cow, it is warm. To keep germs from growing in it, the milk is cooled in a big tank. Next, the milk is pumped into a tank on a truck. The truck takes the milk to a dairy plant.

"Here, the milk travels through hot pipes. It is heated real fast, then cooled right away. This is called pasteurization. The heat kills germs that may make people sick.

"We also learned about cream. Cream is the thick, sweet, fatty part of milk. Before pasteurization, the cream might be skimmed, or separated, out.

cream

milk

"The cream is pasteurized and then many different things may happen to it. Some dairies package the cream or use it to make other things such as butter, ice cream, or cream cheese. When all the cream is taken out of milk, what you have is skim milk.

"If it is not skim, milk is homogenized. This means that some cream stays in the milk. Finally, all the milk goes into cartons or bottles. Machines pour the milk and seal the containers. The milk is then delivered by truck to stores everywhere.

"And that, Billy boy, is where milk really comes from."

Make Your Own Butter

You Will Need:

half-pint of heavy
  (whipping) cream
bowl
mixer
wire strainer
quart of ice water
¼ teaspoon salt
spoon

1. Let the cream sit out of the refrigerator for about an hour. Cream will become butter faster if it is not too cold.

2. Pour the cream into the bowl. Start beating it. In about 5 minutes, little globs of fat will form in the bowl. This is your butter!

3. The liquid left over after the butter forms is called buttermilk. Drain off the buttermilk. You can put it in a glass in the refrigerator to drink later.

4. Scrape the butter from the bowl. Put it in the wire strainer. Hold the strainer over a sink. Slowly pour the ice water over the butter to wash off the buttermilk.

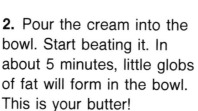

5. Put the butter back in the bowl. With a spoon, mix in the salt. Now, try spreading your homemade butter on hot toast!

*Don't forget to ask your parents for permission.

Instead of using a mixer to make butter, try a jar with a lid. Begin with step 1. Fill the jar half-full with cream. Screw on the lid. Begin shaking the jar. When you get tired, pass the jar to a friend. Your cream will turn to butter in about 20 minutes. Once it does, follow steps 3-5.

A Cheesy Story

There is a legend about an Arab traveler and how he accidentally made the first cheese.

One day, over 4,000 years ago, an Arab traveler—let's call him Hasan—made a trip across the desert. He used a pouch made from a sheep's stomach to store milk for the trip. Using animal parts like this was common back then.

After a long, hot day, the milk had turned into a watery, lumpy mixture. Hasan was curious, and hungry, so he ate it.

Here's what had happened to Hasan's milk: The desert heat and rennin, a chemical found in the stomach of certain animals, acted on the milk. This caused the milk to form soft lumps called curds and thin liquid known as whey (way). Hasan's discovery tasted delicious—it was cheese!

This may not really be how cheese came about. But today, cheese is made much the same way.

A **chemical** is any of the many substances that make up the world, such as water, air, and rocks. Certain chemicals are called enzymes (EHN zyms). An enzyme is a chemical that helps make some other chemicals react with each other and change. In cheese making, the chemical rennin, which is an enzyme, causes the milk to thicken.

In a cheese factory, cheese makers pour milk into big tanks. They warm the milk and then add something called "starter" to make the milk sour. Next they add rennin to make the milk turn into curds and whey.

The curds are heated until firm. The whey is drained off. Then the curds are squeezed to remove more whey.

Machines cut up the curd and press it into molds. The machines also salt the curd.

Most kinds of cheese are then aged at the factory. Some kinds must age for many months in order to have just the right flavor.

What Makes the Holes in Swiss Cheese?

If you've ever blown bubbles into a liquid, such as water, you have some idea of how Swiss cheese is made. Suppose your liquid hardens, but the bubbles stay, as if frozen in place. Something like this happens with Swiss cheese.

Things called bacteria, used in making this special cheese, make the bubbles. As the cheese ripens, the bubbles form. They become the holes you see when the hardened cheese is sliced.

In cheese language, the holes are known as "eyes." The eyes take a few weeks to form within a batch of ripening cheese. Temperatures are controlled so the bacteria will form the eyes just right.

As you might guess, Swiss cheese was first developed in Switzerland. It has been made for over 500 years and demands very special care and skill. Maybe that's why cheese makers consider Swiss cheese the "king of cheeses."

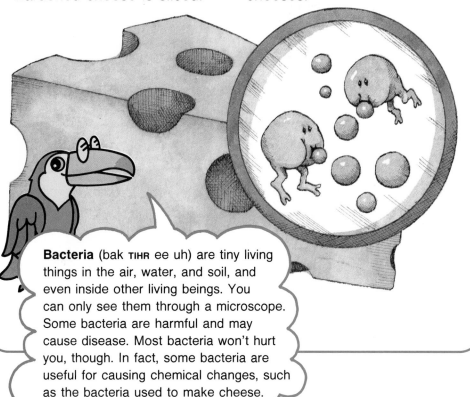

Bacteria (bak TIHR ee uh) are tiny living things in the air, water, and soil, and even inside other living beings. You can only see them through a microscope. Some bacteria are harmful and may cause disease. Most bacteria won't hurt you, though. In fact, some bacteria are useful for causing chemical changes, such as the bacteria used to make cheese.

How the Hot Dog Got Its Name

How did the hot dog get its name? Well, it's *not* because hot dogs are made from dogs!

A hot dog is a kind of sausage. Sausages are made of ground meat that is mixed with spices and stuffed into a casing. The casing keeps the meat together and helps keep the shape of the sausage.

People have been making sausage for several thousand years. During the 1400's, a new sausage was developed: the frankfurter. This sausage was named after Frankfurt, Germany. The weiner is a similar sausage that was named for Vienna, Austria.

When Germans and Austrians came to America, they brought the recipes for weiners and frankfurters with them. In the 1860's and 1870's, these sausages were sold on rolls along the streets of New York City.

People thought these little sausages looked like a dachshund—a long, skinny dog. Salespeople started calling their franks "dachshund sausages."

The name "hot dog" became popular because T. A. ("Tad") Dorgan, a famous cartoonist of the early 1900's, drew some cartoons showing talking and barking dachshund sausages. But he called them "hot dogs." The name "hot dog" caught on and has been used ever since.

Where Do These Foods Come

Study the meals and plants and animals on these two pages. Match each meal with the group of plants and animals from which it was made.

1.

2.

From?

Did You Know?

When making syrup, workers drain the sap from certain kinds of maple trees through spouts that they have tapped into the trees' trunks. Then the workers boil the water out of the sap, leaving a thick syrup. Usually, 35 to 45 gallons (133 to 171 liters) of sap are needed to make just 1 gallon (3.8 liters) of syrup.

3.

4.

C

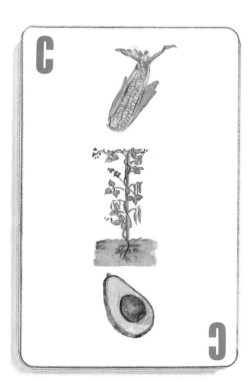

D

Answers: 1-C, 2-D, 3-A, 4-B

These Foods Come From . . .

 is usually made from corn that has been pounded into meal, mixed with water, formed into a flat bread, and then baked or fried. It may also be made from wheat flour.

 are beans that have been soaked, boiled, and mashed. The bean mash is then fried.

 is made using mashed avocados. Avocados are green, pear-shaped fruits grown on trees in areas such as the southern United States and Latin America.

 are potatoes that have been sliced and then fried in oil.

In , the main ingredients are tomatoes, vinegar, and corn syrup.

 is made from the meat of a steer, or male cow.

The is a cucumber before it is sliced and preserved in brine, or salted water.

 is made from the nuts of the cola tree.

 comes from a plant that grows downward into the soil where the peanut pod develops.

 is made from the sap of certain kinds of maple trees.

 is made of berries that grow on vines and of sugar that comes from either a long, tough grass called sugar cane, or from the large, fleshy root of the sugar beet.

 is made up mainly of wheat flour, eggs, and milk. The milk and eggs bind together the ingredients.

 is squeezed from oranges. Often it is made into frozen concentrate, which you mix with water to get your juice.

 is made from wheat ground into flour with stones.

The you find at supermarkets is from dairy cows milked by machines.

Did You Know?
The parts of the peanut plant inside the pod, or shell, are the seeds. These are ground into the oily paste you know as peanut butter.

Tale of the Tomato

One day in 1820, a crowd gathered at the steps of the Salem, New Jersey, courthouse.

"That man is mad!" said one person. "Surely he'll die."

The crowd was watching Colonel Robert Gibbon Johnson do a most amazing thing. He was eating *tomatoes.* In New Jersey in 1820, most people believed tomatoes were poison. But Colonel Johnson knew better. The people of Salem stared as he ate tomato after tomato. They expected him to die, or at least become gravely ill.

To their surprise, when he finished eating he was alive and well. From that day on, the word spread through North America: "Tomatoes are good to eat!"

Today we eat tomatoes all the time. We eat raw tomatoes, canned tomatoes, tomato juice, tomato soup, tomato sauce, ketchup, taco sauce . . . whew! One way or another, the average American eats about 80 pounds (36 kilograms) of tomatoes a year!

Did You Know?
The first ketchups had no tomato in them at all. Many thick, spicy sauces used to be called "ketchup." The name "ketchup" comes from an Oriental word that sounds something like "kaychup." The Chinese made the first ketchup sauce out of pickled fish and spices.

How We Got You, Otis Orange

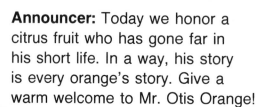

Announcer: Today we honor a citrus fruit who has gone far in his short life. In a way, his story is every orange's story. Give a warm welcome to Mr. Otis Orange!

Otis: You're too kind. Thank you!

Announcer: Otis, we invited friends from your past to join us today. Each one will speak to you from backstage. You last saw the first guest when you left home. Do you recognize her voice?

First Guest: You grew in my grove in Florida. A freeze was coming. So I sprayed your tree and the others overnight. When the water froze, the ice kept the heat inside the oranges and saved them.

Otis: No! It can't be Farmer Joan.

Announcer: Yes, it can. Now listen to this next voice.

Second Guest: Most oranges from the groves go to the factory. They roll in, get juiced, dewatered, frozen until slushy, poured into cans, and then frozen hard as concentrated juice. But Otis was special. He and some other choice oranges were sent to the packing plant. That's where I packed him in a box for shipping.

Otis: Packer Dave, don't tell me you're here!

Announcer: We have more surprises for you, Otis. Listen.

Third Guest: I ran the locomotive that pulled the refrigerator car that carried Otis and his pals. We reached Chicago just two days after the oranges had been picked, fresh as ever.

Fourth Guest: I placed Otis in the produce section at the supermarket. "Yes, ma'am," I said to myself, "this little orange has come a long way."

Otis: Oh my, Casey the Engineer and Babs the Grocer.

Announcer: Otis is so happy, he's crying tears of juice! So long, everyone.

The Big Scoop!

What's your favorite flavor of ice cream? Is it chocolate? Peanut butter? Bubble gum? There are many to choose from. How is it possible that there are so many flavors? The answer is "science." Some ice creams are made with natural flavoring, but others may contain artificial (ahr tuh FISH uhl) flavoring such as vanillin, an artificial vanilla. These artificial flavors are made up in a laboratory by scientists.

Scientists known as flavorists use a machine to separate the various chemicals that make up a food. The flavorists taste and smell these different chemicals to figure out which ones contribute to the food's flavor. For this job, flavorists must have fine-tuned senses of smell and taste. Next, the flavorists mix batches of these chemicals to create an artificial flavoring.

Beans from Flowers?

Natural vanilla flavor comes from beans that grow on a flower called an orchid. Vanilla beans look long and green, like string beans. Curing, or drying, vanilla beans usually takes up to six months and several steps. In one method, the beans are first put in hot water for a few minutes. Second, the beans are spread in the sun during the day and stored in bins at night for several weeks. Third, they are placed on drying frames. The cured vanilla beans are brown and coated with fragrant oil.

flower

beans

Some foods may contain such a small amount of a certain flavor chemical that flavorists may not be able to find it in a laboratory setting. In such a case, they need to work with thousands of pounds of the food to get even a tiny bit of the mystery ingredient. To get a fruit flavor, for example, flavorists go to a jam factory. There they set up huge "nets" to capture the steam as the fruit is cooking. They study the steam to find the missing ingredient.

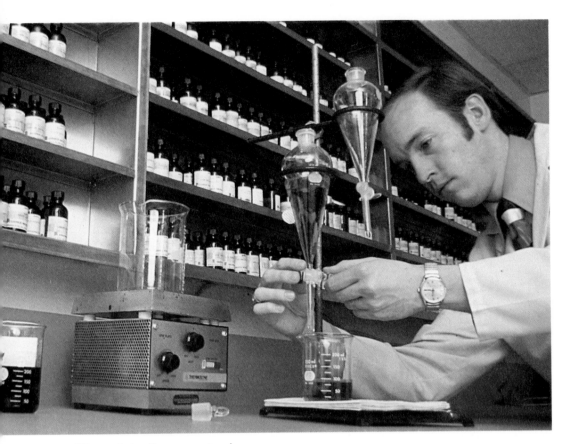

Flavorists figure out where a food's flavor comes from.

Some flavors have escaped even the most clever flavorist. For example, no one has a recipe for a really good artificial chocolate. So most chocolate ice cream is flavored with real cocoa made from cacao (kuh KAY oh) beans.

At a chocolate factory, cacao beans are cleaned, roasted, and shelled. Next, the shelled beans, or nibs, are ground

between stone or steel wheels. The heat from the grinding melts the nibs to form a chocolate liquid. Then the liquid is pressed until it separates into yellow cocoa butter and a light brown cake. Finally, the cake is ground into cocoa. This is what ice cream makers use to flavor chocolate ice cream.

Which tastes better—natural flavorings or artificial? You be the judge. Taste a vanilla ice cream made with natural flavorings and one made with artificial flavorings. What do you think?

Where Does Soda Pop Get Its Fizz?

When you drink soda pop, does the fizz tickle your nose and throat? Do drops of the soda pop come up and hit you on the nose? Here's the story of what makes that fizz.

Many years ago, people thought that bathing and drinking spring water cured some illnesses. This water could be found bubbling out of the ground in certain places.

The demand for this water was so great that scientists tried making it. In 1772, the English chemist Joseph Priestley succeeded. He dissolved carbon dioxide in water. Carbon dioxide is the gas that makes the spring water bubble from the ground. The result was carbonated water.

Soon, this carbonated water was being bottled. Druggists sold it as medicine. They added leaves from different plants to increase the water's healing powers. This also gave the water flavor.

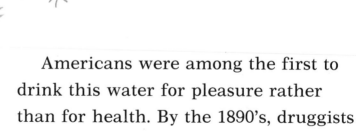

Americans were among the first to drink this water for pleasure rather than for health. By the 1890's, druggists were making many different flavors.

Today, this carbonated water is called soda pop. It is still made much the same way, except it is now made in factories instead of drugstores.

Orange Fizz

1. Fill the glass about one-half to two-thirds full with orange juice.

You Will Need:
medium-size drinking glass
orange juice
1/2 teaspoon baking soda
spoon

2. Add the baking soda and stir gently.

3. Watch as the bubbles rise.

4. Sip your drink and discover the "orange juice pop" taste.

*Don't forget to ask your parents for permission.

Did You Know?

Scientists used bicarbonate of soda, or baking soda, to add carbon dioxide to water. So many people started calling carbonated water "soda." The name "pop" came about because bottles of carbonated water were stopped with corks. When the corks were removed, they made a popping sound.

The Story of Chewing Gum

More than a thousand years ago the Maya, an
American Indian people, lived in a Mexican jungle—

MMMM! The fruit of
the sapodilla tree is
ripe and sweet.

Ah, my blade slipped
and cut the tree! What
is this? A creamy liquid?

The liquid soon thickens
into something like gum,
called chicle (CHIHK uhl).
The Maya discover that
chewing the chicle gives
a refreshing taste.

I must be careful. If I cut too deep, the tree will die or, just as bad, never give chicle again.

In the same jungle today, the descendants of the early Maya collect chicle.

The liquid runs down through the cuts made by the chiclero (chee **KLAYR** oh), or chicle gatherer. It collects in a bucket at the foot of the tree.

The chicleros boil the chicle to remove most of its water.

The chicle is molded into slabs weighing between 20 and 30 pounds (9 to 14 kilograms).

Mules or canoes carry the slabs to planes at nearby airstrips.

The planes take the chicle to ships that sail to manufacturing centers in the United States.

At the chewing gum factory, the chicle is placed in big kettles along with other natural and artificial gums. The kettles melt these ingredients into chewing gum base.

Now for the powdered sugar, a little corn syrup, some vegetable oil, and a dash of cinnamon.

After the gum base is cleaned, it goes to mixing machines. More ingredients are added to sweeten, soften, and flavor it. Some chewing gum is sweetened with sugar, while others have artificial sweeteners.

Other machines cool and knead the gum. Then it is pressed into a wide sheet and sent to the sheet rolling machine.

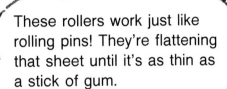

These rollers work just like rolling pins! They're flattening that sheet until it's as thin as a stick of gum.

Next, machines divide the gum into smaller sheets and mark where the sticks will be cut. Other machines break these sheets into single sticks. More powdered sugar may be sprinkled on the sticks, which then sit for a few days before packaging.

Machines wrap the sticks of gum in foil and paper, gather them together, and seal them in a package.

I'm fresh and tasty, thanks to my wrapper.

In a chewing gum factory, machines do all the "hands-on" work. The people never need touch the gum.

Scrub, B!

ush, and Bubble

THINGS THAT KEEP US CLEAN

How does water get to us?

How does toothpaste get in the tube?

What makes a mirror a mirror?

Wilfred Wonders About Water

My little brother Wilfred is always taking things apart. Just today, I saw him go into the bathroom with a tool box. He was working on the faucet when Mom caught him. He said he was just wondering where water comes from.

Mom always knows how to handle Wilfred. She ran around looking for books, paper, and other stuff and called us to the kitchen. "You can put the hammer down, Wilfred!" she said. "I'll *show* you how water gets here." Mom began to draw. I got ready for one of her stories, hoping Wilfred would listen.

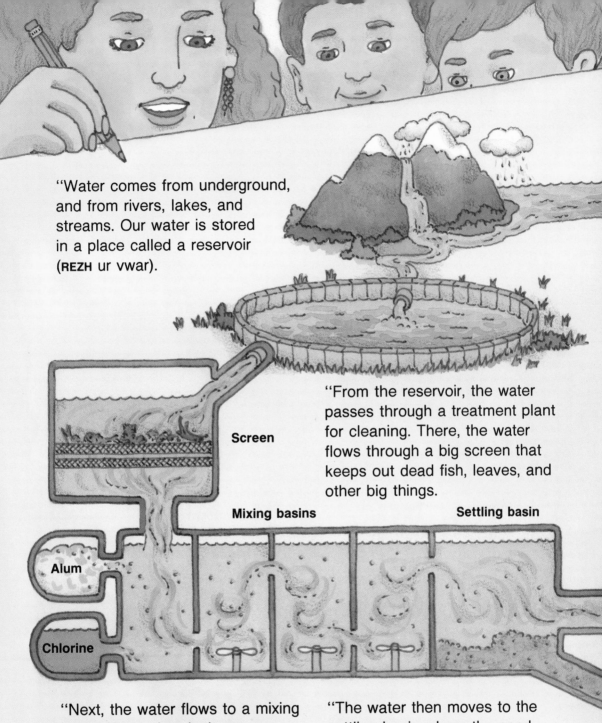

"Water comes from underground, and from rivers, lakes, and streams. Our water is stored in a place called a reservoir (REZH ur vwar).

Screen

"From the reservoir, the water passes through a treatment plant for cleaning. There, the water flows through a big screen that keeps out dead fish, leaves, and other big things.

Mixing basins

Settling basin

Alum

Chlorine

"Next, the water flows to a mixing basin. Here, chemicals are poured into the water to make it safe to drink. One chemical is alum. Tiny bits of dirt in the water stick to the alum. Chlorine is added to kill germs in the water.

"The water then moves to the settling basin where the sand, dirt, and flocs fall to the bottom. Flocs are the bits of dirt that have stuck to the alum. At this point, the water leaves the settling basin . . .

53

Filter

and goes through filters. The filters are made of layers of charcoal, sand, and gravel.

Chlorine

"The water looks clean now, but tiny disease-carrying germs can get through the filters. So, more chlorine is added to the water. Another chemical called fluoride may be added. This helps keep your teeth strong.

Clean water

Pump

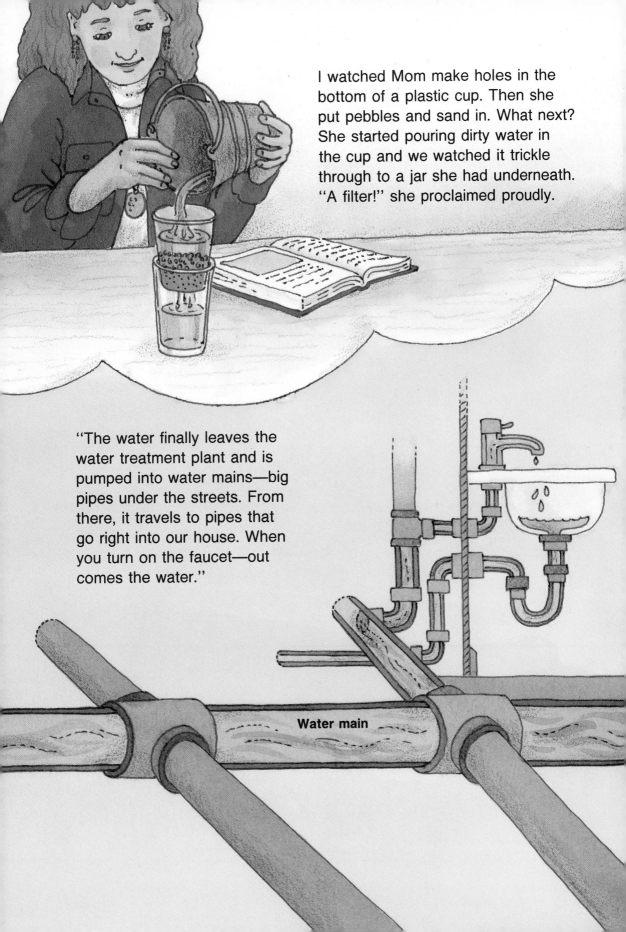

I watched Mom make holes in the bottom of a plastic cup. Then she put pebbles and sand in. What next? She started pouring dirty water in the cup and we watched it trickle through to a jar she had underneath. "A filter!" she proclaimed proudly.

"The water finally leaves the water treatment plant and is pumped into water mains—big pipes under the streets. From there, it travels to pipes that go right into our house. When you turn on the faucet—out comes the water."

Water main

Wilfred slipped away seconds before Mom finished. At first she didn't notice, but then we heard banging coming from the upstairs bathroom. We ran up and there he was, sticking his head out from under the sink. "Now that I know where it comes from, I just wanted to see where it goes," he said with a guilty look.

Mom just laughed and said, "Why didn't you ask?" She continued her story right there in the bathroom.

Sewer

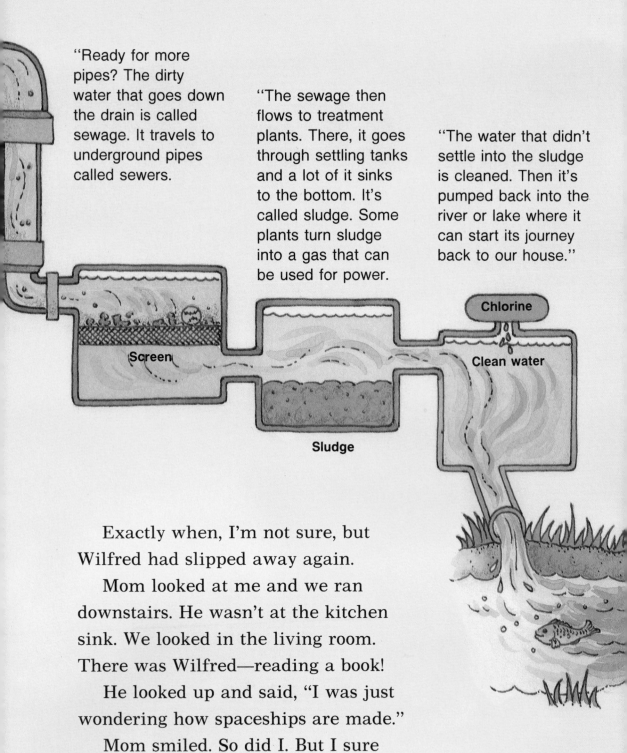

"Ready for more pipes? The dirty water that goes down the drain is called sewage. It travels to underground pipes called sewers.

"The sewage then flows to treatment plants. There, it goes through settling tanks and a lot of it sinks to the bottom. It's called sludge. Some plants turn sludge into a gas that can be used for power.

"The water that didn't settle into the sludge is cleaned. Then it's pumped back into the river or lake where it can start its journey back to our house."

Screen

Chlorine

Clean water

Sludge

Exactly when, I'm not sure, but Wilfred had slipped away again.

Mom looked at me and we ran downstairs. He wasn't at the kitchen sink. We looked in the living room. There was Wilfred—reading a book!

He looked up and said, "I was just wondering how spaceships are made."

Mom smiled. So did I. But I sure was glad we didn't have a spaceship parked in our garage.

Getting soap wasn't always as easy as it is now!

Attack Agents

Watch out! Tiny "surface active agents" are about to surround and attack. Should you be afraid? Not really—maybe you're just about to wash your hands! The tiny agents are chemicals in soap and they "capture" dirt when you wash. Soap surrounds the dirt and then breaks it up into smaller bits. Once the bits of dirt are broken up by soap, water can rinse them away.

How do we get soap? In the early days of our country, people made it at home. They mixed different ingredients and came up with a very dangerous chemical called lye. Then they would boil the lye along with leftover cooking fats in a large kettle. A chemical reaction, or change, took place in the boiling, making something new: soap. When the boiling soap cooled, it would get hard. Then it could be cut into bars.

Today we buy soap, of course. That's a lot easier and safer than boiling it at home! It still has to be made, though. Let's see how.

Dirt Alert

Want to watch soap really go after dirt? Sprinkle pepper into a glass of warm water. Then pour a drop of dishwashing liquid into the middle of the glass. The soap "attacks" the bits of pepper, forcing them to the side of the glass!

One way is to heat fat (usually animal fats or certain vegetable oils) at very high temperatures so that the part of the fat known as the fatty acids separates from the mixture.

Next, an ingredient is added to react with the fatty acids and make something new. That ingredient is caustic (KAWS tihk) soda, another name for lye. The caustic soda mixes with the acids to make soap.

Now the soap is a thick, hot liquid. Colorings are added, and the mixture is vacuum-dried. Imagine a vacuum sucking the water out of the soap to dry it.

Next is the noodle stage. This is where a cutting machine slices up the dried soap into chunks that look like noodles.

Another machine shapes the noodles into "logs" that look something like long loaves of bread.

Our bars of soap are cut from these logs—nice little bars of chemicals ready to attack, surround, and capture dirt!

Soap Paint

You Will Need:

1 cup Ivory Snow
  soap powder
4 bowls
4 tablespoons water
4 spoons for mixing
food coloring
construction paper

1. Pour about ¼ cup soap powder in each of the bowls.

2. Add a tablespoon of water to each bowl. Stir each mixture until thick.

3. Put 3-5 drops of food coloring into each bowl, using a different color in each one.

4. Blend the colors into the flakes. Then roll the different mixtures into soft, soapy chunks and use them as fingerpaints.

*Don't forget to ask your parents for permission.

Upside Down Minerals

Imagine brushing your teeth with snail shells or fishbones! Hundreds of years ago, you may have done so. People have used strange things to clean their teeth. They tried different ingredients, looking for "nature's secret" to clean, strong teeth.

Today we use toothpaste, of course. Toothpaste is made from minerals—calcium phosphates or silicas, for example. Just as in early times, these ingredients come from natural materials, such as shells and rocks.

Other ingredients in toothpaste keep the paste moist and good tasting. Detergents do the actual cleaning, and a chemical called fluoride helps prevent tooth decay.

How do all these different ingredients get into the skinny tube your toothpaste comes in? This mysterious process happens at the factory.

Minerals are the thousands of different nonliving materials found in nature. Rocks are made of minerals. We get many of the things talked about in this book from minerals that you may not have heard of: gel toothpaste is made from the mineral silicate, for example.

First, workers mix the ingredients in a large machine, producing the paste or colored gel. Then the toothpaste is pumped into a funnel-shaped tank connected to the filler, a machine that fills the tubes.

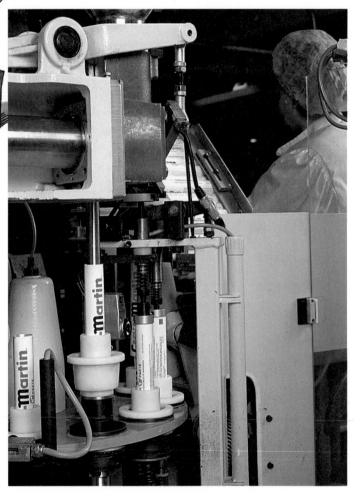

Each tube is dropped cap-side down into a holding cup on a turning table. The caps are on, but the bottoms of the tubes are open. The table turns, and when an electric eye spots a marker on the tube, a nozzle moves down into the tube. The nozzle pushes out an exact amount of toothpaste.

Next the table moves the tube into position for sealing. The ends of metal tubes are folded by a set of mechanical "jaws." Heating jaws seal the ends of plastic tubes. These jaws act like an iron, melting the ends shut.

Now it's time to be pushed out of the holding cups and sent down the line for packaging. Before long, the tubes are in boxes and off to the store where customers can choose their favorite kind.

Minerals, chemicals, and detergents in an upside down tube? When you think about it, we still clean our teeth in a strange way!

A Hog-Hair Toothbrush?

There is a story about an English prisoner named William Addis. Many years ago, around 1780, Addis passed his time making tiny holes in bones he had saved from supper. Then he threaded hairs from a piece of cowhide into the holes and made a toothbrush. Toothbrushes had been around in one form or another for hundreds of years.

But Addis' invention was the first "modern" toothbrush.

Over the next 150 years, inventors tried to improve the toothbrush. But the best bristles were the long hairs of a special kind of hog, and these were hard to get. When a material called nylon (NYE lahn) was developed in the 1930's, companies began to make toothbrushes with nylon bristles. Today, millions of toothbrushes are made each day. Let's take a look at toothbrush making in action.

First we need the handles. Colored plastic crystals are melted and poured into a mold inside a machine. The hot plastic cools in seconds, forming the handles.

Now for the bristles. A worker feeds the handles into another machine, which grabs a bunch of nylon bristles and bends them in half to form a V shape. This machine then cuts off a tiny piece of metal, and quicker than the eye can see, it pushes the metal into the bend in the bristles. Then the metal and bristles are shoved together into each hole of a handle. When the bristles are cut and smoothed, the toothbrush is done.

And so we have millions of toothbrushes a day, in all sizes and colors. Modern toothbrush making would probably surprise Mr. Addis—and make those hogs thankful!

Mirror World

Jenny walks with her grandfather along a woodland path. Suddenly, they see a pond. It is still and clear. As they walk to the edge, Jenny says, "Look. You can see the trees and the sky in the water. You can even see the birds flying overhead."

They step closer and see their reflections in the water. "It's as if our world is down there, looking back at us," says Jenny.

"Like a mirror," noted Grandpa. "And the world looking back at us is the same, only everything's reversed.

If that was your twin we see in the water, she'd do everything you do, only the opposite way."

"You mean," asks Jenny, "in a mirror, right is left, and left is right?"

"Right—I mean correct," answers Grandpa. "That's because light bounces off a mirror before it gets back to you. When it bounces, it leaves the mirror going the opposite way from the way it came. Left turns to right and right to left."

"But how are mirrors made so the glass can do that?"

"Let's look that up when we get home," Grandpa suggests.

Back at the house, Grandpa gives Jenny a book about mirrors. She reads awhile and says, "Long ago, people used to polish metals like gold and silver to make mirrors."

"Isn't silver still used in mirrors?" asks Grandpa.

Jenny continues reading. "Yes. It says here that a silver solution is sprayed on the back of a clean, polished piece of glass. Silver will lose

Mirrors are made from glass, but where does glass come from? Glassmakers blend crushed fine sand with materials called soda ash and lime (from minerals). They heat the mixture until it forms a syrupy liquid. When it cools, it's glass!

Glass

Silver
solution

Copper

Paint

IF YOU WANT TO LEARN, LOOK IT UP!

its shine if air gets to it, so a layer of copper is added over the silver. Then a layer of paint is added to keep air out, just in case."

"Good work, Jenny!" exclaims Grandpa. "Now I have a message for you, but you'll need a mirror to read it." Grandpa winks and says, "I think the message is from your twin who lives on the other side of the mirror."

A **solution** (suh LOO shuhn) is a mixture that forms when you dissolve one or more ingredients in a liquid.

Zip, Snap,

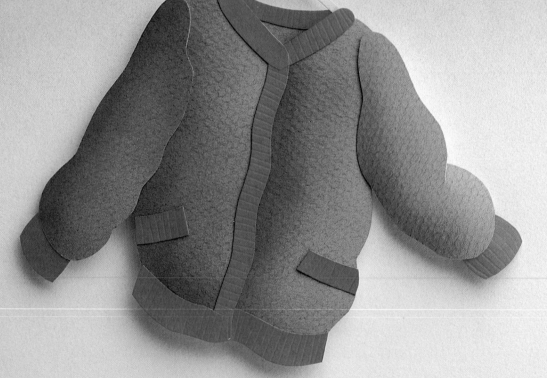

and Button

THINGS WE WEAR

How do we get wool from sheep?

Can cloth come from oil?

Who first thought of sneakers?

What Is It?

To fasten this shoe is easy—
No lace, no knots, no bow.
Small hooks and loops are
    what you see,
For the shoe uses tabs
    of _ _ _ _ _ _ .

This is an item of clothing
Liked by children, adults, and teens.
It's tough, strong, and comfortable.
Everyone wears blue _ _ _ _ _ .

When it goes down, it's open.
When it comes up, it's shut.
A squirrel would find life easy
with a _ _ _ _ _ _ on every nut.

Miss Sheep is soft and gentle,
I sure would like to pet her.
But I think I'll just say thanks
For the wool in this new

_ _ _ _ _ _ _ .

From Sheep to Sweater

When do you wear what a sheep once wore? When you wear a wool sweater, of course! Most clothes made of wool start with a sheep's coat, which we call a fleece. Thousands of years ago, people discovered that wool yarn can be knit or woven into warm, comfortable clothes.

We still take wool from sheep and turn it into sweaters. And the steps are a lot like they were when people made all their own clothes. Machines just make the process faster.

First, the fleece is sheared from the sheep.

Then the wool is washed and carded, or combed, to take knots out. The thin threads of wool, called fibers, are untangled and spread apart into soft, loose strands.

People turn the loose strands into yarn by twisting it and drawing out the ends at the same time. This is called spinning. The earliest spinners spun the fibers between two fingers. American pioneer women used spinning wheels.

A **fiber** is a long strand of any substance, such as cotton or wool. It is at least 100 times longer than it is wide. A fiber can be spun into yarn and made into a fabric for clothes and other things.

Most sheep's wool comes in shades of tannish white. Dyes give it all kinds of colors. In the past, people would use certain flowers, leaves, and other natural materials for dyes. Today we usually get dyes from chemicals.

The two most popular ways of turning yarn into cloth are knitting and weaving.

In hand knitting, you use one or two smooth rods called needles to make loops of yarn go through other loops of yarn. Because of the loops, knitted fabrics stretch easily.

Weaving is done by stretching lengths of
yarn in one direction, and then running
another yarn across them, going over and
under the long threads, back and forth.

Knitted or woven, wool lets us share in
a sheep's "good deal"—and stay warm!

Knitting with a Spool

You Will Need:

large thread spool
   made of wood or
   a plastic you can
   hammer into
four small nails
yarn
hammer
optional: crochet
   hook and blunt
   yarn needle

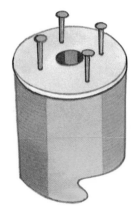

See how knitting works. You can make a knitted cord without needles this way.

1. Have a grown-up help you hammer the four nails into the spool.

2. Drop one end of the yarn through the hole in the spool. Loop the yarn around each nail. Use a clockwise direction around the spool.

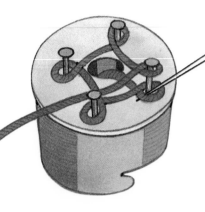

3. When you get back to the first nail, wrap another loop on top of the first loop. Pull the bottom loop over the top of the nail. Make sure the second loop stays on the nail.

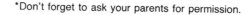

*Don't forget to ask your parents for permission.

4. Keep winding the yarn around the nails. Lift or hook each loop over the nail as you wind. You will be knitting a cord. Gently tug the yarn at the bottom of the spool and you'll see the cord come out here.

5. When you have made a cord long enough, cut off your yarn about 10 inches (25 cm) from the spool. Thread the yarn end through each loop, in order. Use the needle if you want. Last, lift the loops off their nails, pull the yarn end tight, and tie a knot.

6. Wind the cord you knitted to make a place mat. Or use your cord to tie your hair, for a bookmark, or whatever else you'd like.

Cotton is a soft, white puff of fibers. It comes from the boll, or seed pod, of the cotton plant. Picking machines pick cotton from each ripe boll.

From Cotton to Shirt

Think of a piece of cloth as wide as one of your shirts. Then imagine that cloth stretching around the world one hundred times. That's about how much cotton cloth we make in our country each year! What is this stuff called cotton, and how does it get made into your shirt?

Cotton fibers

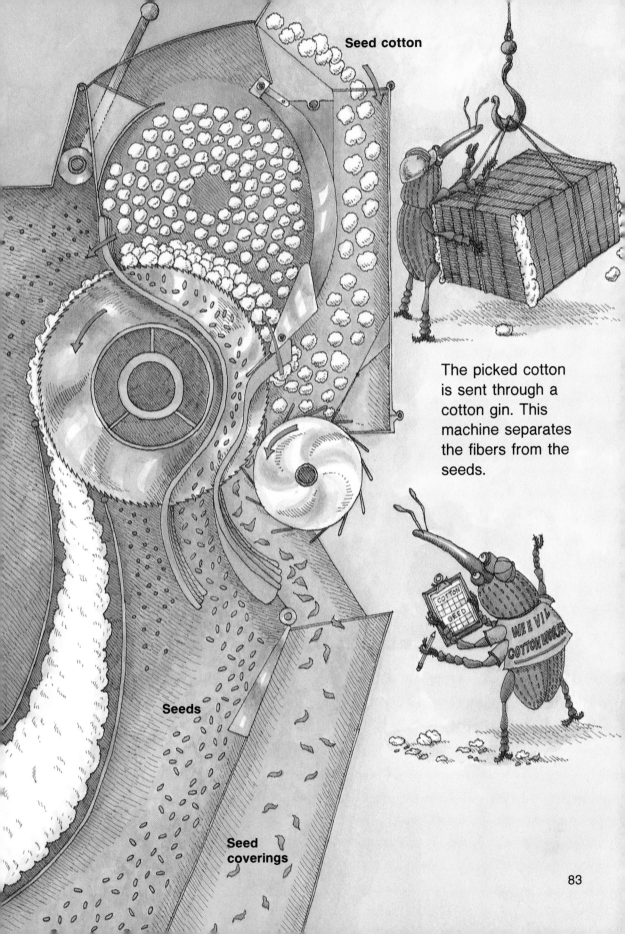

Seed cotton

The picked cotton is sent through a cotton gin. This machine separates the fibers from the seeds.

Seeds

Seed coverings

Next, the cotton is cleaned and sent on for carding. The carding machine uses huge rollers covered with wire teeth to make the fibers lie straight. The fibers go on to spinning machines, which twist and pull the loose yarn into thread.

Now the thread is ready to be made into cloth. It might be knitted into the stretchy kind of cloth used for T-shirts. Huge knitting machines can knit about 12 million stitches in one minute!

Or, the cotton thread might be woven into a firmer, heavier cloth. Weaving machines, which are called looms, work at high speed to turn out this cloth.

What about the colors? Maybe the thread was already dyed before knitting or weaving. If not, the new cloth is cleaned and dyed now, and then it goes on to become your shirt.

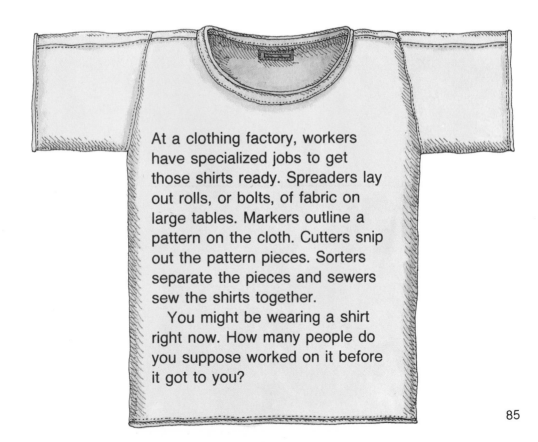

At a clothing factory, workers have specialized jobs to get those shirts ready. Spreaders lay out rolls, or bolts, of fabric on large tables. Markers outline a pattern on the cloth. Cutters snip out the pattern pieces. Sorters separate the pieces and sewers sew the shirts together.

You might be wearing a shirt right now. How many people do you suppose worked on it before it got to you?

Design a T-Shirt

You Will Need:

a plain white T-shirt
a piece of cardboard
   about 12 by 18
   inches (30 by 45
   cm)
permanent markers
plain paper to cover
   cardboard

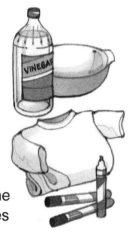

1. First test your markers. On a scrap of white cotton, scribble a square of each color you plan to use. Soak the scrap for an hour in vinegar and water. Then wash it with soap and cold water. Don't use any marker whose color streaks.

2. Fit the shirt over the cardboard. Tape edges down in back.

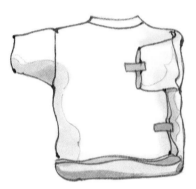

3. Draw your design in pencil on your shirt. If you'll need to erase, draw on paper and tape the paper to the cardboard before fitting the shirt over it. Make sure your drawing is dark enough to be seen when you trace.

4. Use the pointed edge of a marker to trace the outline of your design on your shirt. The color may spread a bit. If you are tracing from a paper, remove the paper as soon as you have finished the outline. (But keep the shirt on the cardboard.) Next, fill in the spaces with the markers' flat edge. When the colors dry, remove the cardboard.

To make your T-shirt last long, soak it in a mixture of vinegar and water. Then wash it with soap and cold water. After this, your shirt can be machine washed.

*Don't forget to ask your parents for permission.

Here's how these marvelous "lockers" work: When you raise the slider on a zipper, you push the teeth together. The ball at the end of each tooth fits into a pocket in the tooth above it.

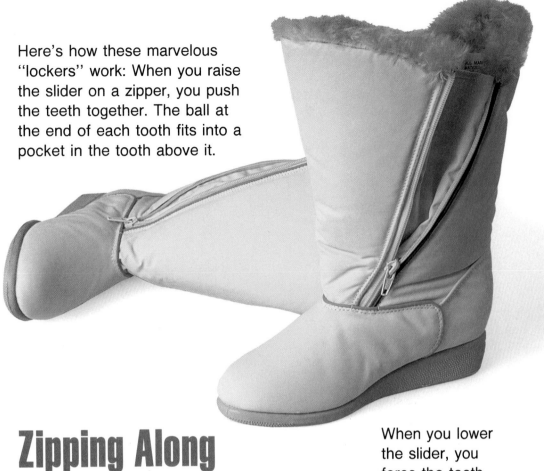

Zipping Along

When you lower the slider, you force the teeth apart again.

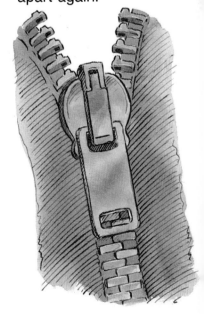

"My clasp locker is stuck!" If you said this about one hundred years ago, maybe you were having trouble getting your shoes on or off. For the Clasp Locker or Unlocker was really the first zipper. It was invented for shoes in 1893.

Zippers, often called slide fasteners in the early days, caught on quickly. The word "zipper" was first used in the 1920's by a company that made zippered rain boots.

How Blue Jeans Started

Would you and your friends care if there were no more blue jeans? Probably! Did you know these famous pants have an unusual history?

The story of blue jeans started when gold was found in California in 1849. Many people rushed there, hoping to become rich by finding gold. Miners worked hard every day, sifting through streams and soil for gold nuggets. Soon their clothes were ragged and torn.

Around 1853, a San Francisco businessman named Levi Strauss had an idea. He decided to make a tough new kind of pants from tent canvas, a heavy cotton fabric.

Miners who tried these new pants liked them because they were so strong. They told their friends how good the pants were. Strauss sold more and more, and then he improved the pants by using another tough cotton called denim.

In 1872, Strauss learned of a tailor named Jacob Davis. Davis was putting metal rivets along the pockets of miners' pants. The rivets made the pants even stronger. Soon Levi Strauss hired Jacob Davis, and they began making and selling riveted jeans.

The pants are still very popular today because they are comfortable and strong. Strong enough to mine for gold? Maybe so, if you ever get the chance!

A **rivet** is a metal bolt that is used to fasten something. The rivets reinforced the pocket seam stitching on the jeans.

Clothes Surprises

These clothes came from a pine tree and an oil well. Did someone just happen to find them in those strange places? Not exactly! Instead, chemists used wood, oil, and other unusual ingredients to make the fibers in the cloth you see.

Look at the synthetic fibers.

All cloth is made from fibers, the long hairlike strands that can be spun into yarn. Some fibers grow naturally, such as those in sheep's wool and a cotton boll. Other fibers are made. We call these **synthetic** (sihn THET ik) **fibers**.

Close-up: Natural fibers

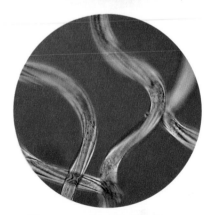

Close-up: Synthetic fibers

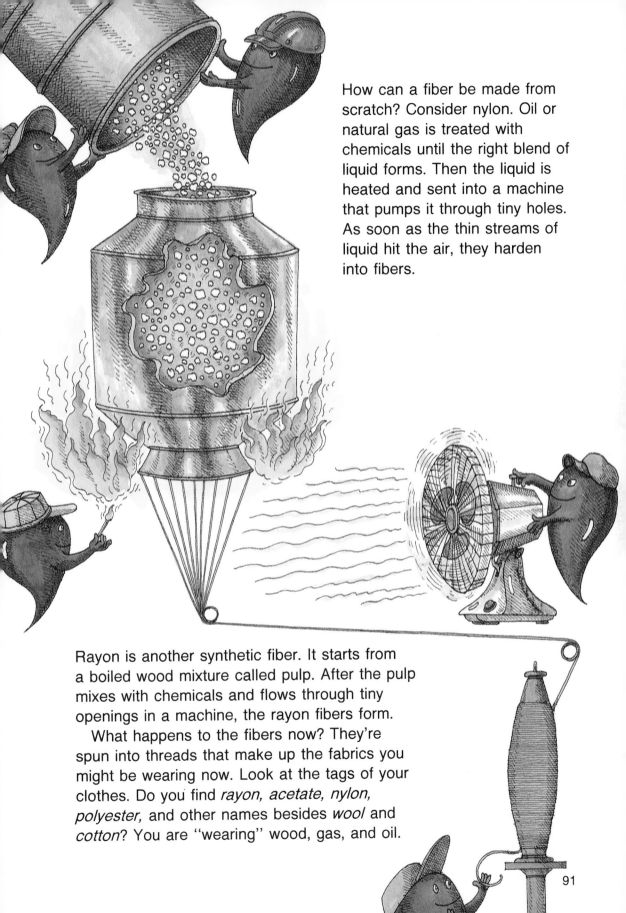

How can a fiber be made from scratch? Consider nylon. Oil or natural gas is treated with chemicals until the right blend of liquid forms. Then the liquid is heated and sent into a machine that pumps it through tiny holes. As soon as the thin streams of liquid hit the air, they harden into fibers.

Rayon is another synthetic fiber. It starts from a boiled wood mixture called pulp. After the pulp mixes with chemicals and flows through tiny openings in a machine, the rayon fibers form.

What happens to the fibers now? They're spun into threads that make up the fabrics you might be wearing now. Look at the tags of your clothes. Do you find *rayon, acetate, nylon, polyester,* and other names besides *wool* and *cotton*? You are "wearing" wood, gas, and oil.

Hooks and Loops

One day in the early 1940's, a man named Georges deMestral took a walk in the woods with his dog. When he got home, he noticed that prickly burs were stuck to his socks and to his dog's fur. DeMestral was curious about why the burs stuck, so he looked at one under a microscope. The bur was made of hundreds of little hooks. It stuck to his socks because they had hundreds of thread loops. The dog's fur also acted like loops.

DeMestral knew that people always need ways of attaching one thing to

another. So he copied the bur's way of
sticking. He made a nylon fastener
with two parts. One part had thousands

of tiny hooks. The other part had
thousands of loops. The hooks attached
themselves to the loops to make a
strong bond. He called his invention
VELCRO*, a combination of the words
velvet and *crochet,* the French word
for "hook."

Now Velcro is on all kinds of
clothes, from sneakers to jackets to
mittens. Do you have some on your
clothes? These tiny hooks and loops
that make fastening so easy will no
doubt "stick" around for a long time!

*VELCRO is a registered trademark for fasteners made by
 Velcro Companies.

The Bouncing Shoe

If you visited some Indians near the
Amazon River in Brazil in the 1700's,
you might think they had funny feet.
That's because they were wearing
rubber on their feet! Rubber is the sap
or milky liquid, called latex, that
comes from a rubber tree. The Indians
dipped their feet in bowls of rubber.
Then they let the rubber dry. These
"shoes" that formed were waterproof

and fit perfectly. They could be called the first sneakers.

However, no one else had rubber shoes. And rubber was not always very useful. It melted in the heat and cracked in the cold. Then, in 1839, a scientist named Charles Goodyear invented a process called "vulcanization" that makes rubber strong, hard, and easy to work with. It made sneakers possible.

In 1868, a sport shoe was made with a rubber sole, a canvas top, and laces. It became known as a "sneaker" because its rubber sole made so little noise. This shoe led to the sneaker we know today.

The rubber parts of the shoe include the *outsole,* or bottom of the shoe. Just above the outsole are as many as nine layers of foam rubber soles to cushion your foot.

Upper

Outsole

So sneakers are pretty new as shoes go, but they haven't stood still! Here's how they're made.

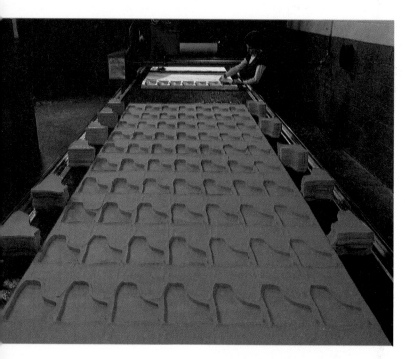

The *uppers,* or tops of the shoes, are cut from canvas. Usually, a different person cuts each of the different parts. He or she operates a *die,* a machine that cuts the canvas like a cookie cutter.

Then other workers sew together all the parts for the upper.

Here, an upper is shaped into a shoe on a metal or plastic form called a *last*. The last gives the shoe the shape of a foot. The shoe gets a bath in latex cement to make sure the parts stay together.

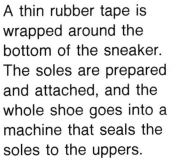

A thin rubber tape is wrapped around the bottom of the sneaker. The soles are prepared and attached, and the whole shoe goes into a machine that seals the soles to the uppers.

Finally, the shoes are tested to make sure they are strong and flexible. An inspector makes sure that the two shoes match, left and right, and are the same size. The inspector may be the fiftieth person to work with that pair of shoes!

Skate, Ped

al, and Pretend

THINGS WE PLAY WITH

Where do crayons come from?

How do we get baseballs?

How can some toys talk and move?

How We Get Crayons

What would we do without crayons? They make the sky blue and the sun yellow in the pictures we draw. But where do crayons come from?

Crayons begin at a place called a color mill. Here, workers mix chemicals to make pigments. Pigments give crayons their color. They can be red, orange, purple—and they can be mixed to make all the colors you can think of!

At the crayon factory, workers mix the powdery pigments with a hot, liquid wax known as paraffin (**PAR** uh fihn).

The colored wax then goes into crayon molds. These are little tubelike openings in this table.

Soon the wax cools and hardens, and the crayons pop out of their molds.

Here the crayons roll into a labeling machine, where each crayon gets its own wrapper.

At last, a sorting machine neatly arranges a rainbow of crayons for boxing. Then the crayons will be into their boxes and off to you! "Ready to color?" a brand-new box of crayons seems to ask.

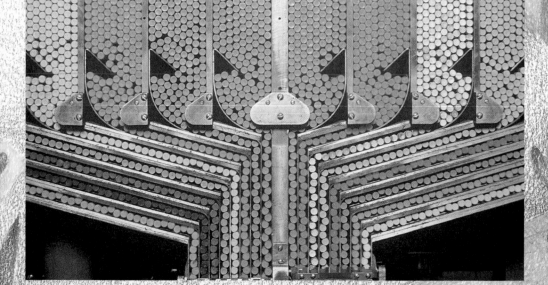

Melted Crayon Pictures

You Will Need:
old crayon pieces, at
    least 2 inches long
    (Fat crayons are
    easier to grate.)
a cheese grater
waxed paper
newspaper
a desk lamp with a
    strong bulb (over
    70 watts)

1. Cover a desk or table with newspaper. This could get messy!

2. Grate different colored crayons into separate piles on the newspaper. Keep your fingers away from the grater!

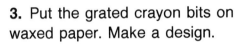

3. Put the grated crayon bits on waxed paper. Make a design.

4. Put another piece of waxed paper over your design.

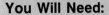

5. Turn on a desk lamp. Place the bulb just a few inches from your crayon design. In about ten minutes, the crayon bits will melt. The waxed papers will stick together. You will have a melted crayon picture!

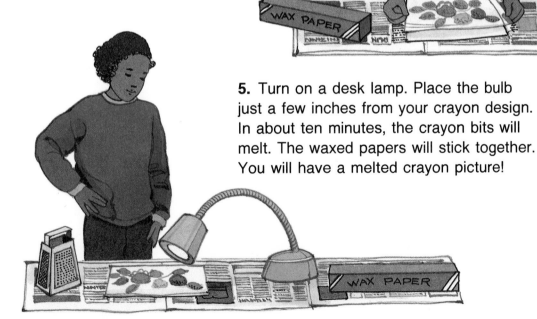

*Don't forget to ask your parents for permission.

A Doll Is Born

"The envelope, please. Ladies and gentlemen, the most popular doll—in fact one of the most popular toys ever produced is . . . " Rip, tear, rustle. "The teen-age fashion doll!"

Surprising? Not if you know the facts. The teen-age fashion doll has been delighting owners for more than thirty years. More than 600 million such dolls have been sold! Where does this star get her start? Let's peek behind the scenes of the toy factory where the doll is made.

Here, the design department creates a model of the doll. Separate molds for the doll's head, body, legs, and arms are made next. Liquid vinyl, a material

made of plastic, is squeezed into the molds. The molds are baked inside an oven. Some doll parts, such as the head, are hollow. These molds are spun around so the vinyl clings to the inside walls. The parts harden as they bake.

Next, the coloring on the doll's face, fingernails, and toenails is sprayed on. A machine stitches synthetic hair to her head. Finally, workers along an assembly line put the dolls together and dress them.

And there she is: All dressed up and ready to go home and play with you!

That's the Way the Baseball Bounces

Did you ever wonder where a baseball gets its bounce? Or why the ball always makes a loud *crack* whenever a batter hits it?

The bounce and *crack* of a baseball are no accidents. Baseball makers take careful steps to make sure every ball is right.

Baseballs start out as small cork balls. Cork is the tough, bouncy bark of the cork oak tree. Cork is light, so that the baseball can fly high in the sky.

The cork center is covered with rubber. The cork and rubber inside the ball make it bouncy. They make the ball go *crack* when it's hit.

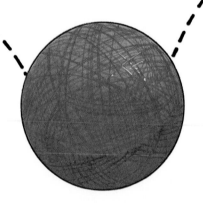

At a baseball factory, machines wrap yarn around the rubber-cork centers to build up their size.

Then the balls are glued to keep the yarn in place. To make the baseball cover, a machine cuts out pieces of cowhide in figure-eight shapes. Workers hand sew two of these pieces together to cover each ball.

Once sewn, the ball is checked for quality. If all is well, it's stamped "official": ready to be pitched, popped up, grounded, or slammed!

Biking It

You might think a bike is simple. You hop on, pedal, and off you zoom! But, really, bikes are quite cleverly designed. Many changes by inventors produced the bikes we know today.

Each part has an important purpose. Look at a bike's frame. The steel tubes of the frame make the bike strong enough to hold you as you pedal.

Do you know why you can ride a bike faster than you can run? It's because of the bike gears. Gears are wheels with teeth sticking out of them.

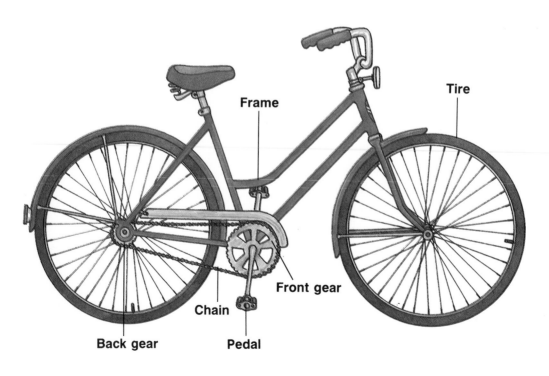

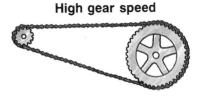

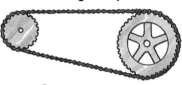

Changing Speeds:

Maybe you have a bike with a gear shift. This means you can change speeds by switching to a different back gear. At high gear speeds, the back gear is small and has few teeth. One turn of the front gear turns the back gear many times. The bike goes fast.

At lower gear speeds, the back gear is larger and has more teeth. One turn of the front gear turns the back gear only a few times. The bike goes slower.

The teeth fit into, or "mesh," with the bike chain. When you push your foot down on the pedal, the pedal turns the large front gear. This gear "drives" the chain. The chain moves a smaller gear on the back wheel. For every *one* time you push down the pedal, the two gears move the back wheel around perhaps *two, three, or more* times.

What if the wheels did not have air-filled rubber tires on them? You would have a rough ride! The air and rubber act like pillows. Tires take the bumps on the road, so that you don't feel them as much.

It wasn't always so easy to hop on and pedal away. Take the "high-wheeler" of the 1870's that some people rode. This early bike had a big front wheel—maybe up to five feet (1.5 meters) high! Riders often leaned their bikes against buildings to climb on and off. If you think it would be hard to keep your balance on a high-wheeler, you're right.

Hitting a stone in the road could throw a rider off.

Today's bike keeps you much more comfortable and safer than that old high-wheeler would. Of course, the rest is up to you. Have fun and ride safely!

"Of course I can handle the high 'high-wheeler,' " this cyclist seems to be saying.

The Tale of the Kite

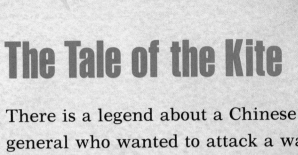

There is a legend about a Chinese general who wanted to attack a walled city. The general planned to have his soldiers dig a tunnel up to and under the wall. Then his army could crawl through the tunnel and into the city.

But how long did the tunnel have to be? To find out, the clever general sent up a kite and marked the string when the kite hovered over the city. The length of the string told him how far to dig the tunnel. The plan worked, and the general captured the city.

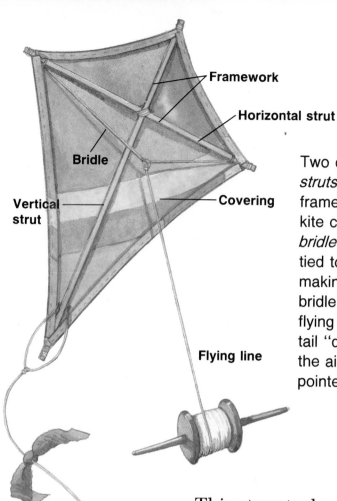

Framework

Horizontal strut

Bridle

Vertical strut

Covering

Flying line

Tail

Two crossing rods called *struts* make up the kite's framework. They hold the kite covering in place. The *bridle* is the pair of strings tied to the sides of the kite, making a "V" shape. The bridle attaches to the long flying line that you hold. The tail "drags" on the kite in the air and helps to keep it pointed toward the sky.

This story took place about 2,200 years ago. Kites have had other starring roles in history, too. In 1752, Ben Franklin flew a kite with a metal key attached during a thunderstorm. Franklin wanted to prove that lightning is electricity. When lightning caused the key to spark, he knew he was right. Others have experimented with kites to test weather conditions and to try out ideas for making airplanes. Mostly, though, kites are just beautiful "aircraft" we fly for fun.

Little Kite

You Will Need:
1 sheet of
    construction paper
scissors
paper punch
paper
    reinforcements
spool of nylon string
1 facial tissue
1 small paper clip
ruler

1. Fold the construction paper in half to measure 6 x 9 inches (15 x 23 cm). Make a diamond by cutting a small triangle off the upper corner of the open edge and a larger triangle off the lower corner of the same edge.

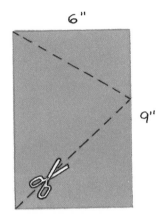

6"

9"

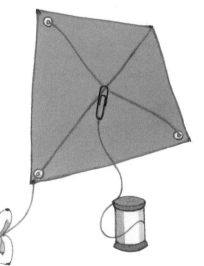

2. Punch holes inside the left, right, and bottom corners of the diamond. Place reinforcements over the holes.

3. To make your bridle, cut a piece of string about 18 inches (46 cm) long. Thread the ends of the string through the holes in the left and right corners of the diamond. In each end, tie large knots to stop the bridle from slipping out.

4. For your tail, cut another string about 20 inches (51 cm) long. Then cut the tissue into four sections. Make bows by gently tying the sections onto the tail string. Leave about 3 inches (8 cm) between each bow. Tie the tail to the bottom corner of the kite.

5. Attach a paper clip to the bridle. Tie the spool of string to the paper clip. Now go fly a little kite!

*Don't forget to ask your parents for permission.

113

The Plastic Family Album

Hi! I'm Plastic Pal. Do you know my family? You should! Plastics are all around you. In one form or another, you use us every day.

Take a look through our family album. Here's our motto:

Versatile! That means we can do or be just about anything.

Here, this is Grandpa Celluloid. In the 1860's, two brothers, John and Isiah Hyatt, made a sticky material by mixing wood pulp and chemicals. Wood pulp is the mushy mixture that is made by boiling chips of wood. The Hyatts' product was soft when heated, but hard when cooled. It was *Celluloid*—the grandfather of plastics!

People made combs, shirt collars, and movie film out of this early

Celluloid. But Grandpa Celluloid had his faults. He burned easily and he cracked.

The first really big success of our family was *Bakelite*. One day in 1907, a chemist, Leo Baekeland, discovered that if he heated certain chemicals under pressure, they would turn hard as a rock. This stuff he called *Bakelite*— a hard, fireproof plastic. It is still used today in telephones, TV's, and cars.

People got excited over how useful Bakelite was. Scientists were soon mixing up many new plastics. They used chemicals made from coal, wood, even milk! They found that chemicals from an oil known as petroleum were especially good for making plastics.

At the plastics factory, workers mix, heat, and process chemicals that came from petroleum. They make basic forms of plastic, called resins (REHZ uhnz). The resins may be bars, rods, sheets, pellets, powders, or sticky paste. The resins are then sent to other factories, to be made into thousands of things.

Factories shape us plastics in many ways. They may use *compression molding*. This is like making waffles. Plastic resin goes in the bottom half of a mold. Then the mold's top half closes down. Heat softens the resin, making it fit to the mold. Then, more heat makes the plastic harden.

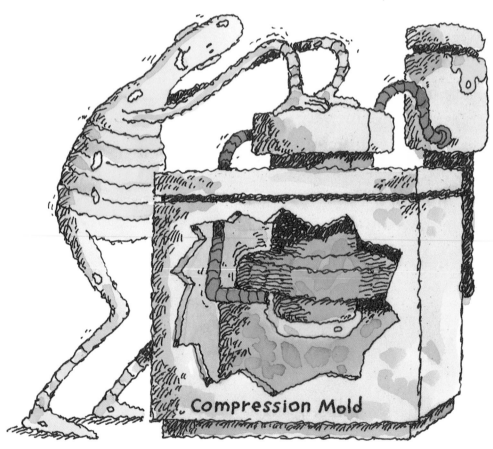

Compression Mold

Blow Molder

Blow molding is another way to shape plastics. A gob of hot, soft resin is dropped into a mold. Then air is blown into the plastic, just like you blow air into a balloon. Bottles and balls are made this way.

Plastic Pellets

Injection Molder

Plastics can also be formed by *injection molding*. The resin is heated into a hot syrup. Then the syrup is squirted into a cold mold, which makes this kind of plastic harden. Many toys are made this way.

The soft, bouncy plastic inside stuffed animals is made by *foam process*. Plastic resin is heated with chemicals to make it bubbly. Then the plastic bubbles are hardened so that they become a firm sponge.

Foam Processor

Now you know some members of the plastics family and how we came to be. See how many of us you can find in your house!

A Good Skate

Coast and glide. Coast and glide. Forward, backward, spin around. Roller skating on today's skates is smooth sailing. Practice for a few hours. Take a couple of spills. Then you're ready to roll with the best of them.

Skating wasn't always this easy. The search for a good roller skate took years. Hopeful inventors were usually devoted ice skaters. They had

to give up their favorite sport each spring when the ice melted. So they tried to replace blades with wheels. One early skate had two wheels, bicycle style, under each shoe. But there was no way to turn or stop. Imagine the crash landings!

Skating became more popular in the late 1800's with new skates that were easier to turn. These skates had a pair of wooden wheels in the front and back of each skate. The wheels were mounted in such a way that skaters

could turn easily just by shifting their weight.

These skates had their drawbacks, too. The straps used for attaching the skates to shoes were uncomfortable and they broke easily. So metal clamps were added to keep the skates on. Skaters tightened and loosened the clamps with skate keys.

Skates kept changing through the years. Sliding soles were made. These could extend to fit growing feet. Wooden wheels gave way to metal ones.

1990

Today, if you have skates, the wheels are probably a strong plastic. They'll keep you gliding for the smoothest, quietest ride yet. The toe stop adds braking power for a safer skate. Comfortable, adjustable straps have probably replaced the clamps. Thanks to all these improvements over the years, you can just keep rolling along!

Get Your Bearings

Some roller skates have little balls inside their wheels. These are called ball bearings. What do they do? Well, bearings keep moving parts turning smoothly. If you have skates, look at the wheels. Do you see the bar that the wheels are attached to? This is the axle. The axle rubs against the small, free-turning bearings in the wheel instead of scraping directly against the wheel. A smoother turn of the wheel means a smoother ride for you.

123

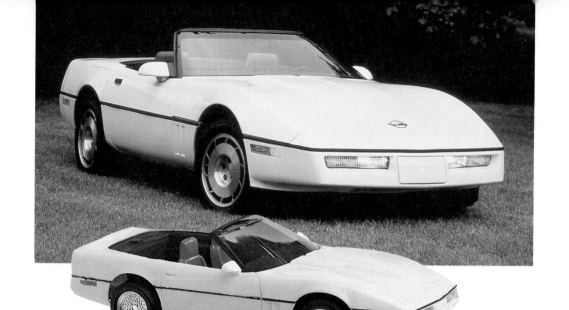

Making a Model Car

"Neat toy car, Pete!"

"Jill, it's a model, not a toy."

"Big difference."

"There is a difference. This model is an exact copy of a 1985 Corvette. Everything the real car has, this one has."

"How is it different from a toy?"

"A toy isn't an exact copy, and it's not made to scale."

"Scale? Like a bathroom scale?"

Pete sighs and keeps on working.

"Just joking," Jill adds. "I know

about scale. One inch is, maybe, 200 miles on a map, right?"

"OK. Only with this model, a half inch equals a foot. It's twenty-four times smaller than the actual car. Even the lights are exactly twenty-four times smaller than the lights on the real car."

"How did the model car people get the pieces to look so real?"

"Well, first they drew a plan to scale from a real car. Next, they carved wooden patterns according to the plan. Then they used the patterns to make molds. They squirted plastic into the molds and let it harden. Presto, they had the parts to my model kit. I did the rest."

"I guess the rest was easy, huh?"

"That's what *you* think. First
I had to paint some parts and fit
all the pieces together—even
these real tiny ones. After that I
glued them. Then I clamped
the seams with tape and let the
glue dry.

"Next, I put putty over the
seams. When the putty dried, I
smoothed it with a file. Now,
I'm painting the rest of the car."

"But what do you *do* with it?"
Pete sighed again at this last
question. "It's just fun to make
things, Jill. Besides, just think
what these hands can do next!"

Jill ran from the room as her
brother chased after her.

Splashing Colors

Sea shell

Coffee

Wax candle

Crocus

Milk

Eggs

What do these things have in common? Give up? They've all been used to make paint. Paint goes back to the time when the earliest people lived on earth. Early people used soot to make black paint. They probably made yellow from crocuses and brownish-reds from clay. These materials were their pigments, or colors.

The first paint makers ground pigments between stones to make powders. Then they mixed the powders with melted beeswax, animal fat, or

Charred wood

127

animal blood. These "binders" made the paint spread and stick on the surface.

Later artists mixed their pigments with water or eggs to get paint. Then in the 1400's, European painters began using oil as a binder. In early America, settlers made paint from the things

Making New Colors

Early painters did not have to find a plant or mineral to make every color they wanted. Instead, they often mixed pigments to make new colors. You've probably mixed red and blue paint to make purple, and yellow and blue to make green. But what colors would make olive or russet? Match the following samples of these colors to the right combinations below.

Olive

Russet

they had, such as milk and coffee grounds. Next, resins were added to make the paint harden and last longer. Natural resins are sticky liquids that come from some trees or from insects. Shellac is an example of a resin.

Today, paint factories follow many of the same steps that paint makers always have. They mix the pigments with binders and resins for the poster paints you use. But they can make up hundreds of gallons (liters) at a time. Let's see how it's done.

Yellow paint coming up! But, first, workers have to make the pigments in a color mill.

First, pigment, binder, and water mix in a huge tank called a high-speed disperser. Powerful blades spin around and around to spread the pigment evenly through the paint. At this stage, the paint is a paste.

Next the paste flows into smaller tanks where more binder and water are added. Afterward, the workers check the paint for quality and color. If all is well, the paint can be packaged. Now it's ready for you and your brush!

Making Paint

1. Scrape about a teaspoon of powder from the piece of charcoal into the bowl (or get the powder from the bottom of a bag of charcoal).

2. Mix the powder with the safflower oil. This is your paint.

3. Paint a small picture on the drawing paper. Note the time when you finish painting.

4. Every hour or so, touch your painting to see if it has dried. Note the time when it finally passes the touch test.

Variation: Try mixing more charcoal powder with different binders: an egg yolk, an egg white, or a teaspoon of milk or water. Make a picture with each new paint you make. Time how long it takes each one to dry and compare the different colors you get.

*Don't forget to ask your parents for permission.

Amazing Chips

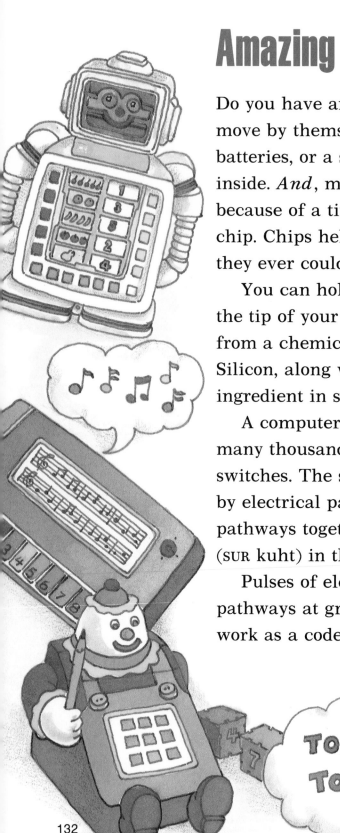

Do you have any toys that talk or move by themselves? Maybe they have batteries, or a small tape cassette inside. *And*, maybe your toy works because of a tiny, amazing computer chip. Chips help toys do more than they ever could before.

You can hold a computer chip on the tip of your little finger. It is made from a chemical element called silicon. Silicon, along with oxygen, is the main ingredient in sand.

A computer chip is packed with many thousands of tiny electrical switches. The switches are connected by electrical pathways. All the pathways together form a circuit (SUR kuht) in the chip.

Pulses of electricity move along the pathways at great speed. These pulses work as a code, telling the chip what to

132

Would you like me to tell you a story?

do. Electrical signals enter and leave the chip along thin strands of wire.

Suppose you turn on a doll that has a computer chip inside it. Electricity races out of a battery along a wire to the chip. The electricity moves through the chip, making switches open and close. The doll opens her eyes, her head turns to look at you, and her mouth moves as she says, "Would you like me to tell you a story?"

Computer chips work the same way to make other toys talk. Have you ever seen a toy computer that said words or numbers? The toy can talk because of a speech synthesizer (SIHN thuh sy zuhr). To "synthesize" means to "put together."

Sounds are put together so they sound like someone talking. Take the word "book," for example. One signal from the computer chip tells the synthesizer to make a "b" sound. The next signal from the chip says "make an 'oo' sound." Then there's a signal for a "k" sound. The sound runs together to make the word "book."

Where do chips for toys get their start? Designers map out their pathways and switches on large paper patterns. When finished, the large patterns will be shrunk down and carved on the chip. Other people plan the signals the chip will get, the ways it will open and shut its switches, and the signals it will send. Part of this

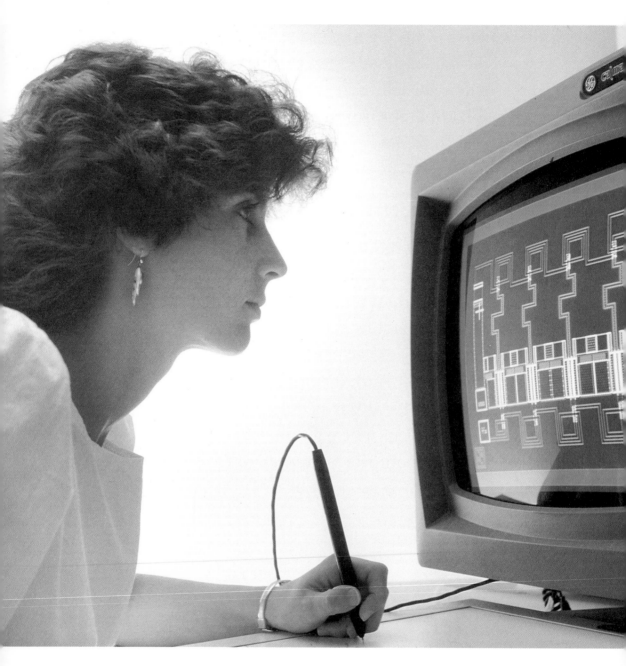

Let's see, what does this chip have to do
next? Chip designers use computers to help
them map out the circuits in the chips for
other computers and computer toys. Every
single action or sound a computerized toy
makes needs long, complicated planning.

information is built into the chip, and part is sent to it as electrical signals after it is made. The chip will have all the directions a toy needs to talk, dance, or roll its eyes.

So hurray for the smart little computer chip! It helps bring toys to life.

Batteries

If the computer chip is the "brain" of a moving, talking toy, the battery is its "heart." The battery sends electric energy along the wires inside the toy.

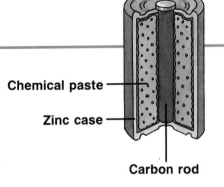

Chemical paste

Zinc case

Carbon rod

Inside one typical kind of battery is a can made of the metal zinc. In the middle is a rod made of a chemical called carbon. Between the rod and the zinc case is a paste made of other chemicals.

When the toy is turned on, chemical reactions in the paste and the zinc free the electric energy stored in the battery.

An electric current flows up the carbon rod to a wire connected to the top of the battery. The current travels along the wire through the toy. On the way, it makes the toy move or talk. Then the current flows from the wire back into the bottom of the battery. In time, the zinc in the battery is slowly used up. In other words, the batteries wear out.

Read Writ

Writenn

e, and "Enter"

THINGS THAT HELP US LEARN

Where does chalk come from?

How does "lead" get inside a pencil?

How do we get books?

How does a calculator count?

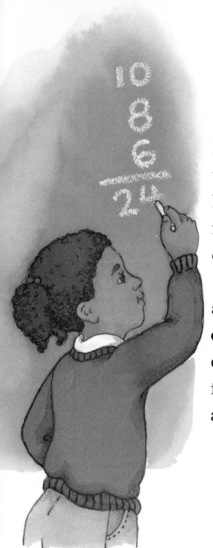

How We Get Chalk

Do you remember the first time you wrote on a chalkboard? It was fun holding a big piece of chalk. If you made a mistake, it was no trouble to erase and try again.

You already know a few things about chalk. It's white or pastel-colored. It breaks easily. And it's dusty. That's because chalk is made from soft minerals: calcite (KAL syt) and gypsum (JIHP suhm).

In a chalk factory, workers mix ingredients, just like in a recipe: calcite or gypsum, water, and clay or a powder known as plaster of Paris. They use a huge mixing machine. For pastel chalk, they would add colored powders.

Next, the chalk mixture is forced out of the machine through a narrow opening. It comes out looking like sausage-shaped tubes. Or, it may be poured into molds that form it into the shape of the chalk sticks we use.

If you like baking cookies, you'll see that chalk is baked in much the same way. The tubes are cut into sticks, or the chalk is emptied from the molds. The cut or molded pieces slide into an oven on trays. Then the chalk bakes for about six hours.

When the sticks are cool, they are counted by machine and put into boxes. By the time it gets to you, the chalk is ready for anything: from giving you a writing assignment on the chalkboard to just playing hopscotch or tic-tac-toe!

Plaster of Paris is made by heating gypsum. Why is a famous city in the name for this "powder from gypsum"? Because many gypsum mines are found near Paris, France.

141

Homemade Chalk

You Will Need:

2 tablespoons
   plaster of Paris
   (from a craft or
   hardware store)
2 tablespoons water
small plastic
   sandwich bag
paper cup
mixing spoon
2 clothespins
clothesline or hanger
optional: food
   coloring

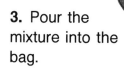

1. Mix the water and plaster of Paris in the paper cup.

2. Mix in a few drops of food coloring if you wish.

3. Pour the mixture into the bag.

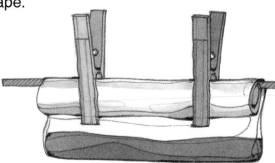

4. Roll down the top edge of the bag, molding the mixture into a tube shape.

5. Clip the closed bag to a clothesline or hanger. Keep the tube straight.

6. Wait a day for the plaster to harden. Unwrap your chalk and let it dry another day or so before using.

142

*Don't forget to ask your parents for permission.

Wooden Sandwiches

When is a lead pencil not a lead pencil? When it's made from graphite (GRAF eyt). Long ago, people did use sticks of lead to write, but we no longer use it. Graphite is a soft mineral that comes from underground mines. A pencil is really a strip of graphite inside a stick of wood. Here's what happens:

A graphite mixture—graphite, clay, and water—blends together in a huge tank. Then the mixture flows into a machine and comes out in the form of sticks that look like licorice.

The strips of graphite-clay mix are cut into pieces and baked in a hot oven. Then they're dipped in wax after cooling. The wax helps the pencil write smoothly on paper.

Cedar is an ideal wood for pencils because it is soft. That makes it easy to sharpen. First, cedar logs are sawed into thin slats. Then the slats are stained, waxed, and dried.

Next, machines cut narrow grooves in each slat. After glue is spread over one slat, the graphite-clay strips are placed in its grooves, and another slat is pressed tightly over it.

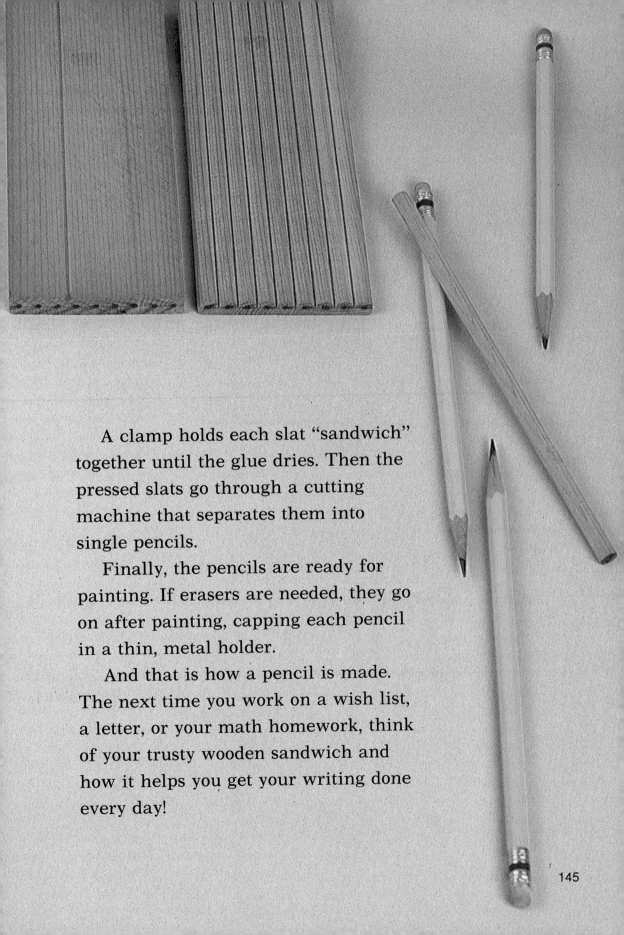

A clamp holds each slat "sandwich" together until the glue dries. Then the pressed slats go through a cutting machine that separates them into single pencils.

Finally, the pencils are ready for painting. If erasers are needed, they go on after painting, capping each pencil in a thin, metal holder.

And that is how a pencil is made. The next time you work on a wish list, a letter, or your math homework, think of your trusty wooden sandwich and how it helps you get your writing done every day!

Cooking Wood for Paper

Tear a small piece of tissue or newspaper. Look at it closely. If you use a magnifying glass, you'll see tiny fibers on the torn edge. Under a microscope, the paper fibers look like a bundle of straw that was pressed flat.

The fiber in paper is called cellulose (SEHL yuh lohs). It is found in plants. All the plant foods you eat contain cellulose. So does the paper in this book—but don't try eating it! The cellulose in paper comes from trees. Here's what happens.

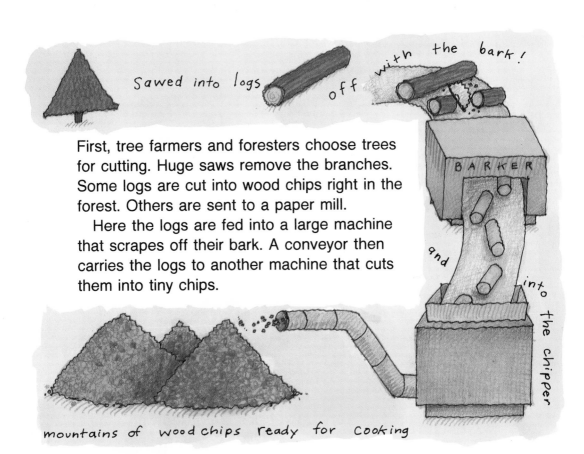

Sawed into logs off with the bark!

First, tree farmers and foresters choose trees for cutting. Huge saws remove the branches. Some logs are cut into wood chips right in the forest. Others are sent to a paper mill.

Here the logs are fed into a large machine that scrapes off their bark. A conveyor then carries the logs to another machine that cuts them into tiny chips.

BARKER

and into the chipper

mountains of wood chips ready for cooking

Piles and piles of wood—ready to become paper

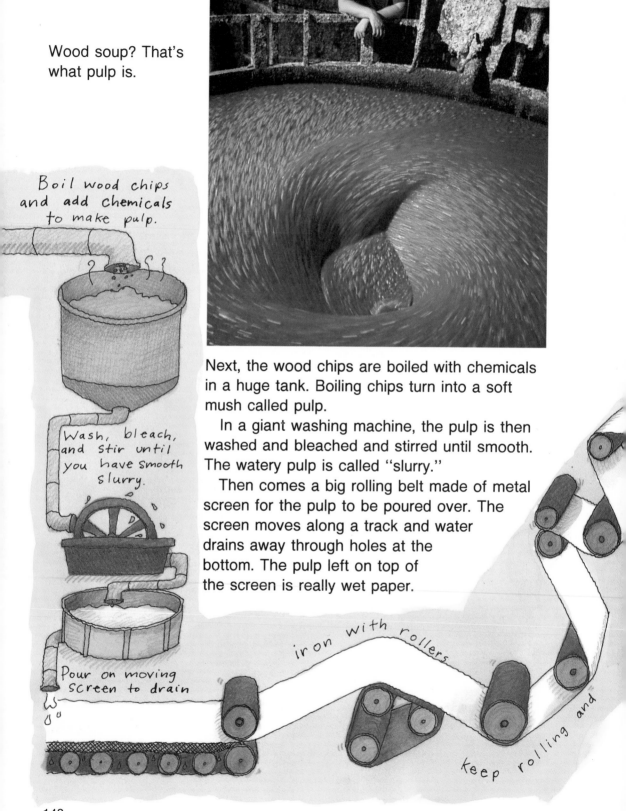

Wood soup? That's what pulp is.

Boil wood chips and add chemicals to make pulp.

Wash, bleach, and stir until you have smooth slurry.

Pour on moving screen to drain

iron with rollers

keep rolling and

Next, the wood chips are boiled with chemicals in a huge tank. Boiling chips turn into a soft mush called pulp.

In a giant washing machine, the pulp is then washed and bleached and stirred until smooth. The watery pulp is called "slurry."

Then comes a big rolling belt made of metal screen for the pulp to be poured over. The screen moves along a track and water drains away through holes at the bottom. The pulp left on top of the screen is really wet paper.

Now for the super ironing process: The wet paper flows between huge rollers that squeeze water out of it. Then it passes over and under heated rollers that dry the paper further. Still more rollers press and smooth the paper surface.

rolling

until dry

Will we always have enough trees to give us paper? We hope so! Recycling paper is one way to avoid wasting trees. See if your city has a recycling center. From here, old paper is sent back to the mills. Then it can be boiled down and made into new paper.

When the paper is dry, it is wound up in huge rolls before being cut into sheets. The rolls can reach as high as the second floor of a building!

Recycled Paper Square

You Will Need:

3 facial tissues
hot water
bowl
hand beater
square baking pan
rolling pin
newspaper
¼ cup of liquid
  starch
wire screening,
  edges folded, to
  fit in pan
dishtowel

1. Tear up the tissues in small pieces, about the size of postage stamps. Drop them into the bowl and add a cup of hot water.

2. Beat the mixture until it's smooth, with no big pieces. This is your "slurry."

3. Stir in the liquid starch. Then pour the mixture into the pan.

4. Dip the screen into the pan, sliding it under the slurry. Move the screen around to get a thin, even layer of slurry on top. Use your fingers to distribute the mixture.

*Don't forget to ask your parents for permission.

5. Lift the screen straight up out of the pan and allow water to drain off.

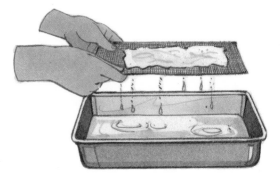

6. Lay the screen between sheets of newspaper.

7. Use a rolling pin over the newspaper to blot your paper.

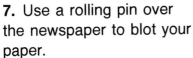

8. Turn the screen over and gently lift your paper off the newspaper.

9. Let your homemade paper dry on the dishtowel for a day or so.

How Ideas Become Books

It feels good to open a book. You flip through the pages, and the words and pictures invite you along for adventure. Or, they help you find things out.

How do we get books?

They start with ideas.

The writer, or author, has a good idea for a story or a factual book. He or she writes to a publishing company about the idea, or maybe even sends a whole manuscript.

A **manuscript** is a typed copy of an author's book. To publishing companies, the manuscript is the material that will be set into type.

When the manuscript is finished, a copy editor checks the manuscript for mistakes. Copy editors also check for mistakes in spelling or punctuation.

Proofreader Marks
≡ capital
paragraph
⊙ period
∧ insert

If so, the editor and author will talk. The editor will probably suggest changes to the manuscript along the way.

An editor decides if the book will be interesting for others to read.

A designer figures out how the book will look by making a layout, or plan, of each page.

Now the manuscript is "marked up," or coded, for typesetting. The codes tell how the words should look when they're printed.

The marked-up manuscript is ready to go.

An artist or photographer will make the pictures for the book.

The manuscript is typed into a computer at a typesetting company or right at the publisher. The long pages that come out are called galleys.

The artist sends pencil drawings of the pictures first, to be sure they're right.

Proofreaders read one set of the galleys and use special marks to show any errors. Final pages of type are then made in the form of film.

Meanwhile, a machine called a scanner "sees" the book pictures and makes their images in film. This film is combined with type film to make printing plates. These are thin sheets of metal that are exposed to light when pressed against the film. The plates pick up the film images this way, and they're then used to print the book.

The designer cuts up one copy of the galleys and uses it to make a "dummy" of the book. The dummy shows exactly how the words and pictures will look on pages.

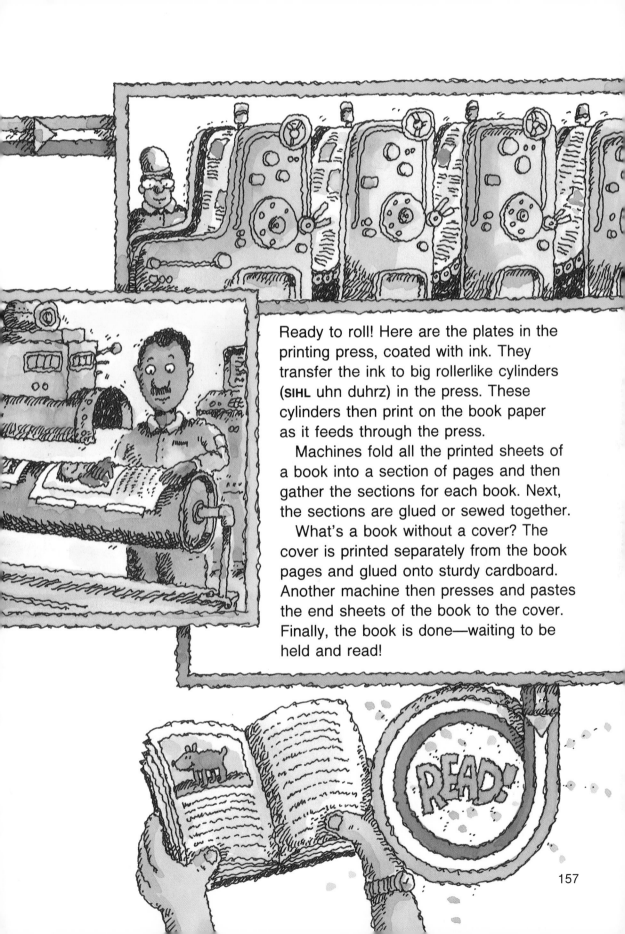

Ready to roll! Here are the plates in the printing press, coated with ink. They transfer the ink to big rollerlike cylinders (SIHL uhn duhrz) in the press. These cylinders then print on the book paper as it feeds through the press.

Machines fold all the printed sheets of a book into a section of pages and then gather the sections for each book. Next, the sections are glued or sewed together.

What's a book without a cover? The cover is printed separately from the book pages and glued onto sturdy cardboard. Another machine then presses and pastes the end sheets of the book to the cover. Finally, the book is done—waiting to be held and read!

Counting Machines

It's a little machine that can tell you how many baseball cards you're missing. Or, perhaps, how much money you got for your birthday. What is it? A calculator, of course! It's really a tiny computer that helps you count and work arithmetic problems.

How did we get calculators? They came along after other kinds of counting machines. One of the earliest of these was the abacus (AB uh kuhs), a frame with strings of beads. The beads stand for whatever you might be counting.

Suppose you were a shepherd long ago counting sheep with an abacus. For each sheep you counted, you'd move a bead on the first (far right) string to the top of the frame. On the abacus shown here, each bead on the second string stands for ten. Each bead on the third string stands for one hundred, and so on.

Later "adding machines" had levers to pull and buttons to push. More recently, inventors used electricity and electrical switches in machines for counting.

Inside a calculator there are thousands of tiny electronic switches. They're called transistors and are linked together along pathways called circuits.

A switch has only two positions, on or off. So if you press or "enter" *1*, the ones switch turns on. But if you enter *2*, the twos switch turns on, and the ones switch stays off, because the twos switch shows *2* all by itself.

Our shepherd would have known that two sheep plus one sheep equals three sheep. But let's see how a calculator "thinks" this through:

When you enter *2 + 1*, the calculator turns on the twos switch, and then it turns on the ones switch also.

Now other switches take over. They know that when the ones switch and the twos switch are both on, the number *3* should light up in the display panel. There you see your answer, whether it stands for three sheep, baseball cards, or dollars!

With old adding machines, you had to "crank" out the numbers.

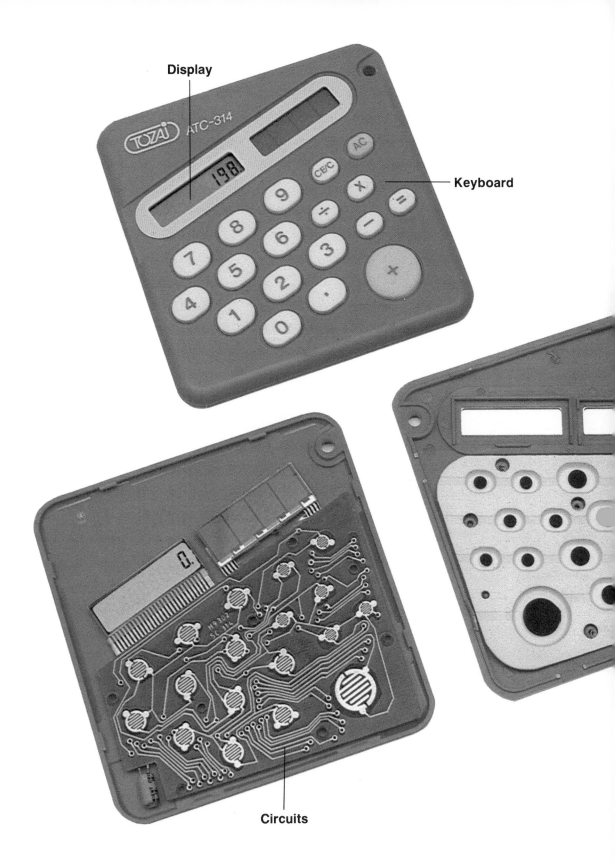

Display

Keyboard

Circuits

Smart, Fast, Ready to Obey

Do you ever play computer games? If so, you know a lot of things computers can do. They ask questions. They tell if your answers are right or wrong. They keep your score, and they might even say "Good-by" when you're done. It's almost as if someone were inside these marvelous machines, working with you. How did computers get so smart? It's because of the way they are made.

The computer's "brain" is its main chip. The main chip follows the

MAIN CHIP

MEMORY BOARD

You can't see them all here, but the memory board packs thousands of memory chips for the computer to process information.

step-by-step instructions known as the computer's program. The computer's main chip can do math, like a calculator. It also acts like a police officer directing traffic. The main chip can control the flow of electric signals from one part of the computer to another. Other, "memory," chips help out the main chip. They can give information the main chip needs in the form of electric codes.

Do You Remember?

A computer chip is that tiny piece with all the switches and pathways. It's much smaller than a dime. Electric signals move through the chip, in and out along tiny wires. They obey orders and bring orders to other parts of the computer.

How does the computer get information for playing a game, for example? It has to be told. One way is through the keyboard. This has the buttons with letters and numbers that you press. Or the computer can read a disk you put into it. Although you can't see them, there are lots of tiny spots on the disk that the computer reads as a code.

The computer's screen shows the information the computer gives us. If you've played computer games, you know how fast the pictures change.

This is because computers work at lightning speed. The main chip of the computer can do millions of jobs in one second. Each job is very small: opening or closing one switch, sending an electric signal along a wire. But all together, they can be amazing!

You might say that computers are so smart because they take orders so well. Every time you put a disk in a computer, you are saying "Let's play a word game." or "Let me see how fast I can think out these math problems. Work with me." And your friend inside is always ready to obey.

Calls, Ca

rds, and Letters

THINGS THAT KEEP US IN TOUCH

How does your phone get its ring?

Where do stamps come from?

How do letters get to your mailbox?

After spilling acid, Alexander Graham Bell sent the first telephone message, calling for help.

Funny Phones

The first phone didn't look or work like the phones used today. If you spoke into it, you couldn't hear anyone answer. The first phone could only transmit, or send, messages. But it was very important because Alexander Graham Bell used it when he sent the first telephone message in 1876 to his assistant: "Mr. Watson, come here. I want you!"

Earliest box phone

The first phone sold in the United States looked like a box with a cup on the end. Later phones were attached to the wall and had a cup for speaking and a handheld receiver for listening.

Desk phone, about 50 years ago

Eventually, phones were made so they had a receiver that was used both to talk and to listen. Today's phones are still made this way. And they have dials or push buttons and use electricity to let you make a phone call.

Phones have come a long way since Alexander Graham Bell's day. Today, you can choose a phone from a variety of colors, shapes, and sizes.

Inside a Phone Call

What happens when you phone someone? Find out on a trip into the phone.

Your trip begins in the receiver. When you lift the receiver, or handset, of your phone, it sends electrical signals on wires from your house to the phone company.

The numbers you dial tell the phone company's equipment to connect your phone line with your friend's. An electrical signal makes her phone ring.

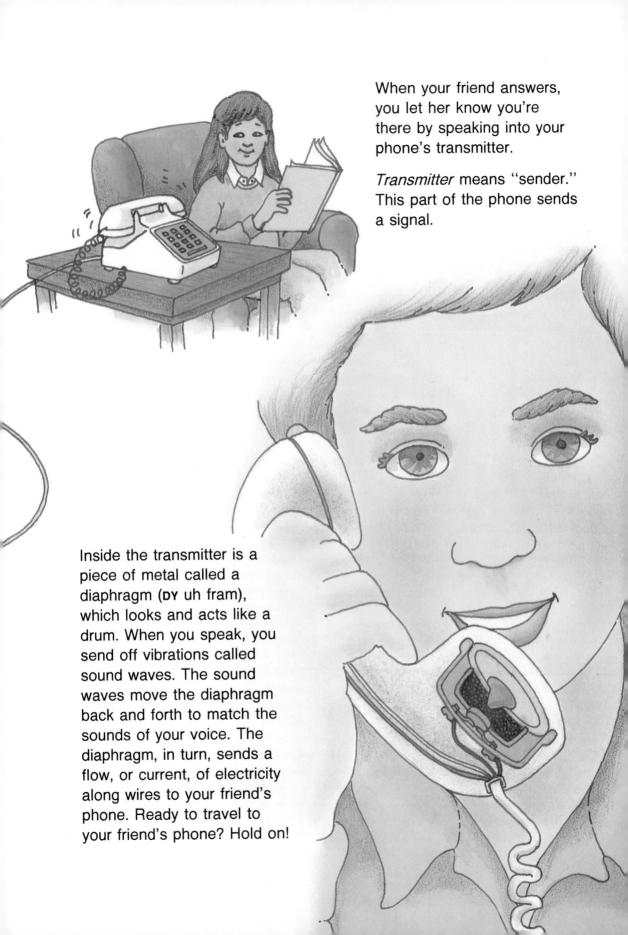

When your friend answers, you let her know you're there by speaking into your phone's transmitter.

Transmitter means "sender." This part of the phone sends a signal.

Inside the transmitter is a piece of metal called a diaphragm (**DY** uh fram), which looks and acts like a drum. When you speak, you send off vibrations called sound waves. The sound waves move the diaphragm back and forth to match the sounds of your voice. The diaphragm, in turn, sends a flow, or current, of electricity along wires to your friend's phone. Ready to travel to your friend's phone? Hold on!

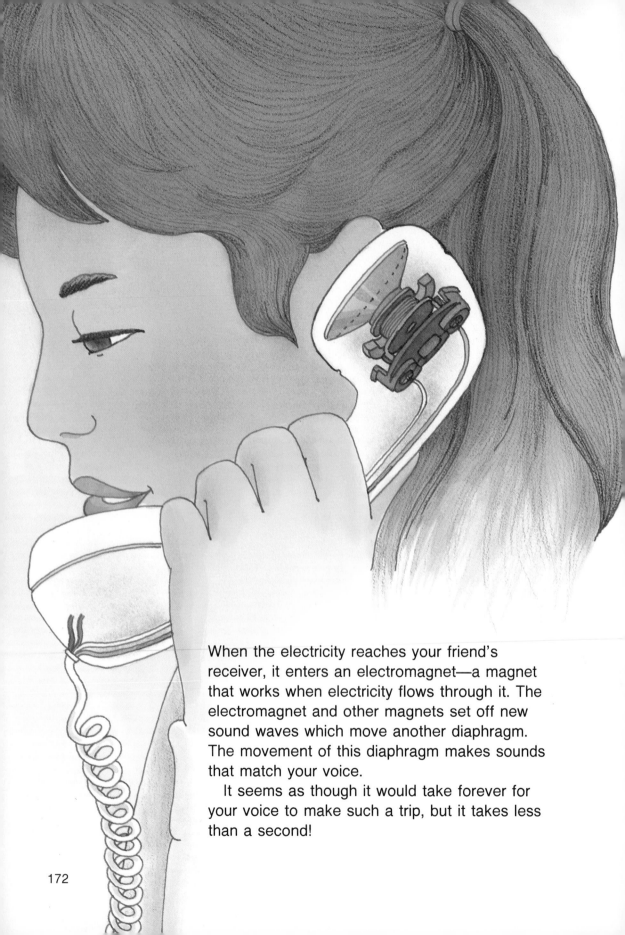

When the electricity reaches your friend's receiver, it enters an electromagnet—a magnet that works when electricity flows through it. The electromagnet and other magnets set off new sound waves which move another diaphragm. The movement of this diaphragm makes sounds that match your voice.

It seems as though it would take forever for your voice to make such a trip, but it takes less than a second!

Phones That Talk and Write and . . .

Of course phones are for calling and talking to people. But today, they can do much more. And in the future, you can bet that they will do even more. Here are some of the amazing things phones can do.

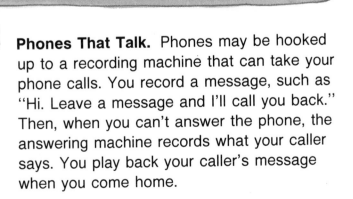

Phones That Talk. Phones may be hooked up to a recording machine that can take your phone calls. You record a message, such as "Hi. Leave a message and I'll call you back." Then, when you can't answer the phone, the answering machine records what your caller says. You play back your caller's message when you come home.

Phones That Write and Draw.

A facsimile (fak SIHM uh lee), or fax, machine allows you to send words and pictures over phone lines. You put a page with a message on it into one fax machine and dial the number of the fax machine that you want to receive your message. Your machine changes the message into electrical signals that travel over phone lines to the receiving fax machine. That machine changes the signals back into your message and prints a copy.

FAX TO YOU

Phones for Deaf People.

A Telecommunication Device for the Deaf, or TDD, allows deaf people to use phones. Almost all TDD's work by having both the caller and the person called type messages. The deaf person can read the messages and respond.

Phones That Travel.
Cordless phones let you go around the house, even outside, while you're on the phone. These phones have a base that is connected to phone lines, and a handset, which sends radio signals to the base. Radio signals are electric signals sent through the air.

When you call a friend from a car phone, radio signals are sent to a nearby station that has an antenna. Next, the call goes to a switching station. Finally, it goes to the phone company that sends it to your friend's phone.

Phones for Computers. A modem is a phone that lets computers "talk" to each other. With a modem, you can send a lot of information from your computer to another computer in minutes, even if it is far away.

Phones and Television. Phones can carry television signals, too. Some businesses have teleconferences in which several people, all far away, can see each other as they talk.

Stamping It

Birds of the air . . .

REPUBLIC OF MALDIVES

1 L

Fregata arieli iredalei

creatures and plants
of the sea . . .

Coral Reefs USA 15c

Chalice Coral: American Samoa

UMM AL QIWAIN

AIR MAIL

3 RIs

and all sorts of
life on land appear
on postage stamps.

RETICULATED GIRAFFE

GIRAFFA CAMELOPARDALIS RETICULATA

RARE ANIMALS

KENYA 50 CENTS

PALAU
22

GECKO *(Gekko vittatus)*

USA 15c

Seeing For Me

People star on stamps, too. You can find inventors, explorers, healers, and other famous and not-so-famous people on stamps.

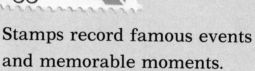

Stamps record famous events and memorable moments.

Stamps are tiny windows onto the world.

At one time, a person getting mail usually paid a letter carrier for delivery. In 1840, Great Britain introduced a penny stamp that a sender bought and placed on a letter. The stamp was like a receipt, as if saying, "Deliver me. My sender has already paid for the service."

Benjamin Franklin

The United States Post Office was set up to organize the mailing of letters and packages. In 1847, it introduced stamps as a way of paying for mail service. Two stamps came out at this time. One pictured Benjamin Franklin, the first postmaster general. The other showed George Washington, the first President of the United States.

George Washington

Making a new stamp begins with an artist creating a design. Next, someone takes a picture of the design, reduces the picture to stamp size, and etches, or cuts, it into pieces of metal called plates.

Many copies of the design are etched next to each other to fill the large plates. Finally, the plates are mounted on presses and millions of stamps are printed. In fact, if all of the stamps made in one year were laid end to end, they would circle the world 25 times!

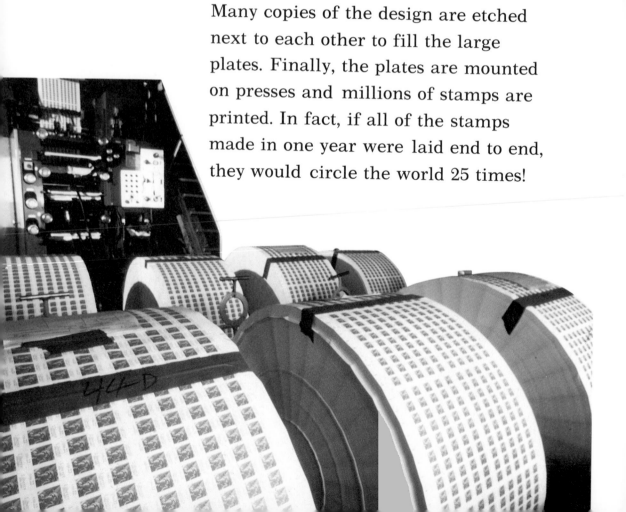

Starting a Stamp Collection

How can you learn about history by looking at tiny pictures? By collecting stamps. All you need are stamps, an album to keep them in, and some tools for handling them.

Did You Know?

A stamp collector is called a *philatelist* (fuh LAT uh lihst). This name comes from two Greek words, *philos*, meaning *loving*, and *atelos*, meaning *paid*. A person who collects stamps shows a love of stamps, and stamps are proof that a person has paid to send a letter.

Stamps. Save stamps from letters or buy new ones from the post office. For a fast start, buy batches of stamps—mixtures of a hundred or more.

Albums. There are albums made just for storing stamps. Some show stamps grouped by country or by topic. If you like, you can make an album out of a scrapbook or notebook.

Tongs and Hinges. Use tongs to handle your stamps and hinges to hold them in place in your album. Hinges are small pieces of paper to which you attach your stamps. This way, you glue your stamps to a hinge instead of to a page in your album, allowing you to move your stamps around.

More Tools. As your collection grows, you may want other tools, such as a magnifying glass for seeing tiny details in your stamps. You can learn more about your stamps from stamp catalogs. The more you know about your stamps, the more fun you can have!

Make Your Own Stickers

You Will Need:
1 envelope
  unflavored gelatin
1 tablespoon cold
  water
3 tablespoons very
  hot water
½ teaspoon corn
  syrup
small bowl
paintbrush
small, homemade
  address label and
  "sticker" pictures
1 envelope
a letter you've
  written

1. Pour the cold water into the bowl. Sprinkle the gelatin over the water. Watch it wrinkle up. This will take about ten minutes.

2. When the gelatin is soft, add the hot water and the corn syrup. Stir until the gelatin dissolves.

3. Brush the mixture over the backs of your address labels and sticker pictures. Let dry.

4. When the glue is dry, moisten it—lick the pieces or use a little water. Place the address label in the upper left corner of the envelope. Use the stickers to decorate the letter and seal the envelope flap.

5. Now your letter has a personal touch. Don't forget the real sticker: the stamp!

*Don't forget to ask your parents for permission.

How Jill's Letter Got to Samantha

Jill was having a great time at camp, but she missed her best friend from back home, Samantha. She decided to write her a letter. On the envelope, she wrote Samantha's name, street address, city, state, and ZIP Code. Then Jill put

a stamp on the envelope and dropped it into the camp mailbox.

Later that morning, the mail carrier drove into camp, delivered several letters, and picked up Jill's letter and all the other letters from the mailbox. He took them into the post office in the nearby town.

There, clerks separated the local mail from the mail going out of town. That mail went by truck to the nearest major mail processing center.

Did You Know?

ZIP Code is a system used to speed the delivery of mail in the United States. ZIP stands for **Z**oning **I**mprovement **P**lan. ZIP Codes have nine numbers. Each number tells post office workers where the different pieces of mail should be delivered— which state, which city, and which neighborhood.

At the processing center, clerks separated the packages from the letters.

Jill's letter went on to a machine that sorted all the letters by size. Then it went to a machine that first turned the envelopes so they all faced the same way. Then it canceled the stamps by printing lines on them so they could not be used again.

Next, batches of letters, including Jill's, were sorted according to ZIP Codes.

Jill's letter went into a large tray with the other letters going to her hometown. The tray was put into another truck.

Some trucks carried letters to the airport, to be flown far away. But the truck with Jill's letter drove straight to the post office in her hometown.

There the letters were sorted according to the last numerals in the ZIP Code, and sorted again according to the mail carriers' routes.

The next day, the carrier who delivered mail on Samantha's street dropped a letter into the mailbox in front of Samantha's house. But it didn't stay there long!

Clay-Print Stationery

You Will Need:

tempera paint or ink
small bowl
modeling clay
construction paper

1. Pour the paint or ink into the bowl about half-full.

2. Shape the clay into a simple design, such as a diamond or heart. You may also press a design into the clay surface.

3. Dip your clay design into the paint or ink to cover the surface of your design.

4. Press the paint-covered clay against your paper and let it dry.

5. To make a new design, wash off the clay and reshape it.

*Don't forget to ask your parents for permission.

Pop-Up Greeting Cards

You Will Need:

stiff paper, such as
    poster board
pencil
construction paper
ruler
crayons or markers
scissors
a picture you have
    drawn and cut out,
    or one cut from a
    magazine or used
    card
glue

1. Cut a strip of stiff paper about 6 inches by 1 inch (15 centimeters by 2.5 centimeters). Using a ruler, find the center of the strip and mark it. Draw lines at ½ inch (1.3 cm) and 1 inch (2.5 cm) from each end.

2. Fold the strip back, away from you, at the center, and at each line.

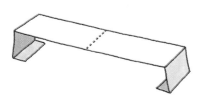

3. Fold a piece of construction paper in half. Place the strip across the inside fold so that the center of the strip is lined up with the center of the folded construction paper. Glue the tabs.

4. Fold the picture exactly in half as shown. Glue it to the strip.

5. Write your message on the front of the card and around the picture.

*Don't forget to ask your parents for permission.

Cartoons, Speci

TV, and al Effects

THINGS WE WATCH

Do cartoons really move?

How do all those people "get in" the TV?

How can you get a picture from a
piece of black tape?

Cartoons—Moving Cels?

Elephants fly! Mice sing and dance! Coyotes fall off cliffs and never get hurt! Anything can happen in a cartoon. Watching a cartoon is like looking into another world.

It's hard to believe that the lively "world" of cartoons is just a lot of flat drawings. Cartoon characters do not really move and talk on their own. They seem alive because of *animation* (an ih MAY shuhn). This is a way of making still pictures appear to move.

192

Say you are a cartoon maker and you want to show a ball rolling down a hill. First, you would draw a ball at the top of the hill. Next, you would draw the picture again, with the ball just beginning to roll away. You would draw many pictures—each new one showing the ball a bit farther down the hill.

Then a camera would shoot the pictures, one at a time, in order. Now the rolling ball pictures are on a strip of movie film. They can be shown very fast, one after the other, in a movie projector. To the people watching the movie, it doesn't look like lots of different pictures of a ball. It looks like one ball rolling.

The cartoon shows you see on TV are made at animation studios. There, writers think of an adventure some cartoon characters can have. They make a *storyboard*, which shows the story in pictures and tells what the characters say.

In a recording studio, actors read the characters' words into microphones. Their voices are put on tape. Then workers add music and noises, such as footsteps, to the tape. This is the sound part of the cartoon show.

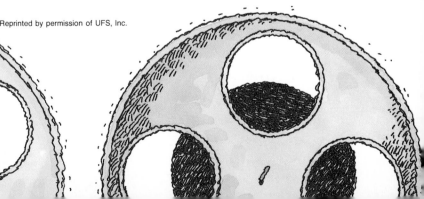

Next, artists work on what you see in the cartoon. Some artists draw only the backgrounds. This might be the trees or houses that the characters appear in front of. Other artists draw the characters themselves.

Still other artists copy the cartoon characters on sheets of see-through plastic called *cels*. Painters color the cels. Some studios have computers that color the cels. Many different cels are needed to show just one move a character makes.

Each clear cel is placed on a background drawing. Then its picture is taken, using movie film. For every minute of action in the cartoon, camera workers have to shoot almost 1,500 cels.

For the whole story, that means thousands of cels are put together. And what you have is one delightful cartoon that makes you laugh.

Cartoon Flip Book

You Will Need:

small, pocket-sized
   notepad
pencil

Here is an easy way to make
your own cartoon at home.

1. Think of a simple action
you want to show, such as
an arrow going into a
valentine heart.

2. Decide how long you
want your cartoon to be. You
could use 10 or even 20
pages of the notepad. How
many drawings do you want
to make?

3. Start your cartoon on the
last page of the notepad. Say
you want to show an arrow
moving toward a heart. First,
draw the heart at one end of
the page and the arrow at
the other.

4. On each of the following
pages, draw the heart in the
same place. But draw the
arrow a little closer to the
heart each time. On the last
few pages, draw the arrow
going through the heart.

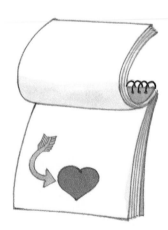

5. Flip through the pictures
and see your cartoon.

*Don't forget to ask your parents for permission.

Special Effects: Making People Fly

What would it be like if people could fly? Actually, some people do—in the movies, that is. You've probably seen them in fun movies, such as *E.T.: The Extra-Terrestrial*.

Well, people in movies don't really fly. But moviemakers know tricks to make actors look as if they do. These and other special tricks used in movies are *special effects*.

Here is one way an actress rises off the ground: She wears a harness under her clothes. The harness is attached to strong, thin wires, painted a color that makes them hard to see.

The wires go up to pulleys and then down to machines that lift the actress into the air. The movie camera is aimed to show the actress, but not the pulleys.

To make her flight seem more real, wind machines blow around the actress's clothes and hair. "Whooosh!" noises are added to the movie's sound track.

To make "fliers" look as if they are in the sky, moviemakers do some *superimposing* (soo per im **POZE** ihng). First they film the sky, showing clouds or stars moving fast. Then the two films are put together as one. The image of the person is put (superimposed) on the sky.

Even when you know how people "fly" in the movies, it's still fun to watch!

Screen Creatures

In movies, you see monsters, witches, creatures from outer space, and other strange folks. Where do screen creatures come from? Is there a place where they all live?

The place where the weird creatures really live is in the minds of moviemakers. The people who make movies think: What will make people stare in wonder? What kinds of funny creatures will make them laugh?

Makeup artists can make monsters out of the nicest people using putty, a fake eye, face paint, and a wig.

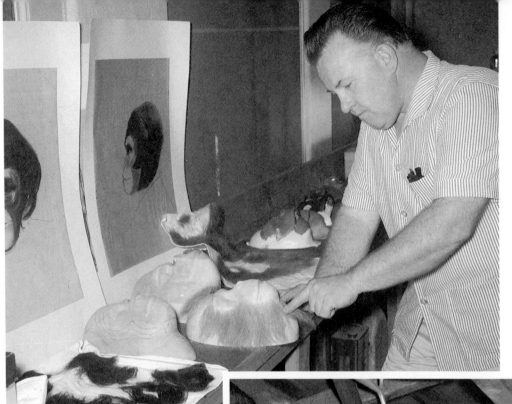

Sometimes they make rubber monster masks for people to wear.

Other times, they make monsters out of cloth and fur and plastic. Some of these monsters are puppets. Some have machines inside them to make them move. Some are so complicated that a computer has to tell the machine monster how to move.

Some movie creatures are just little clay or rubber models. A camera trick makes them seem alive. First, the camera takes a picture of the model in one pose. Next, a worker moves the model's arms and legs, just a little. Then the camera takes the creature's picture again. All the many moves of the model are filmed this way. When people see the movie, they don't see a person moving the model. It looks as if the creature is moving by itself.

Robots from the movie *Star Wars* need a little help to get their acting right!

The camera makes
the models look
bigger than they
really are.

How do moviemakers make a
creature taller than a mountain?
Simple. They just make the mountain
very small!

However they're made, one thing is
for sure: You'll never see creatures like
these in real life. They're part of the
amazing, make-believe world of the
movies!

Tuning In

Funny clowns hop along. Colorful floats glide by. Drums roll and trumpets blare. It's a parade and it's "live" right on your TV screen.

How does the telecast get to you? Is it as "easy as one, two, three"? Not exactly, but three things do have to happen for that parade to show up on your set.

First, a TV camera with a microphone has to take the picture and sound and turn them into electricity. Second, electric signals blending picture and sound signals have to be transmitted, or sent, to your set. Third, your set has to turn the signals back into a scene that you can see and hear.

The camera lens focuses the light from the scene you are watching. Mirrors inside the camera reflect the light and split it into three primary colors: red, green, and blue. All the colors you see on your TV screen are made by mixing red, green, and blue.

A tube in the camera changes the light into electricity. You can't see

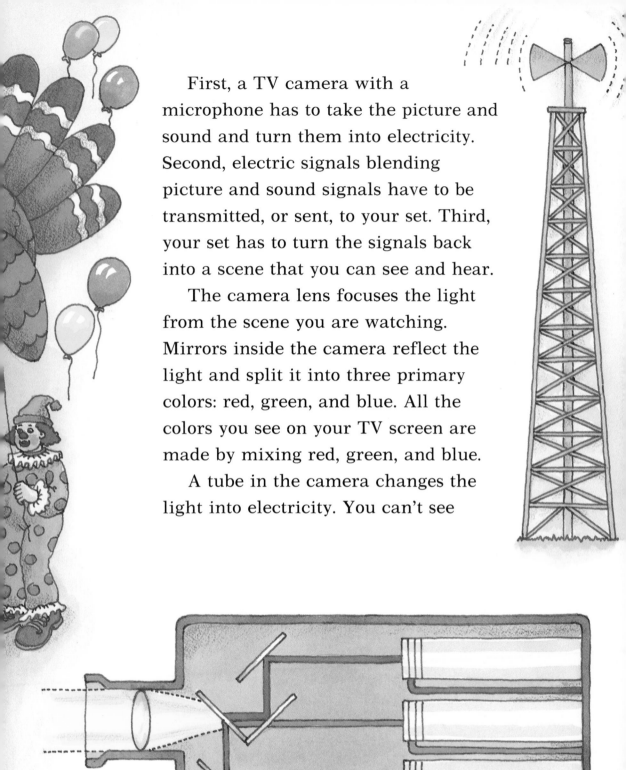

them, but electric signals will become
the pieces of the picture and the sound
being televised to you.

These signals, called waves, travel
through the air from a TV broadcast

antenna. A series of antennas or instruments called satellites can carry signals long distances.

Your TV antenna receives the signals and sends them into the set. Once inside, the speaker and the picture tube turn the signals into the sound and light patterns that just entered the microphone and the TV camera. And the parade marches on, live, before your eyes!

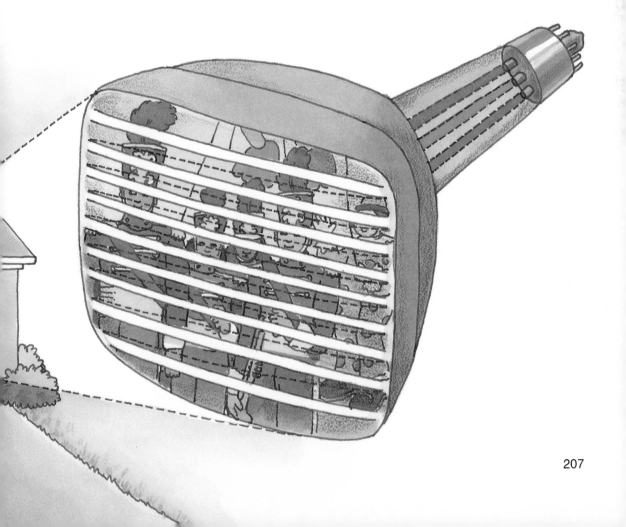

How We Get Videotapes

Slide the tape in, press a few buttons, and you can have your favorite TV show taped while you're out playing baseball. A videocassette recorder, or VCR, can receive television signals and store them. You can watch a movie or other show even when it's not really "on" TV.

Here's what happens. The VCR uses
a plastic tape coated with very tiny pieces of
a kind of iron metal. When the tape is
recording signals, or playing them back, rods
called loading posts pull part of the tape out
of its case, called a cassette. They bring the
tape in contact with parts of the recorder.

The tape starts on a supply reel
and goes to a take-up reel. Both
reels are inside the cassette.

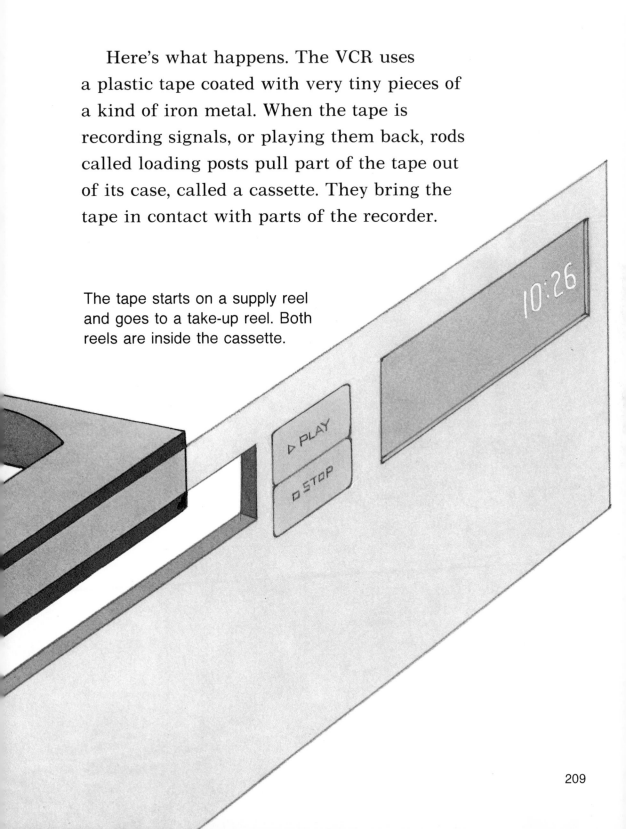

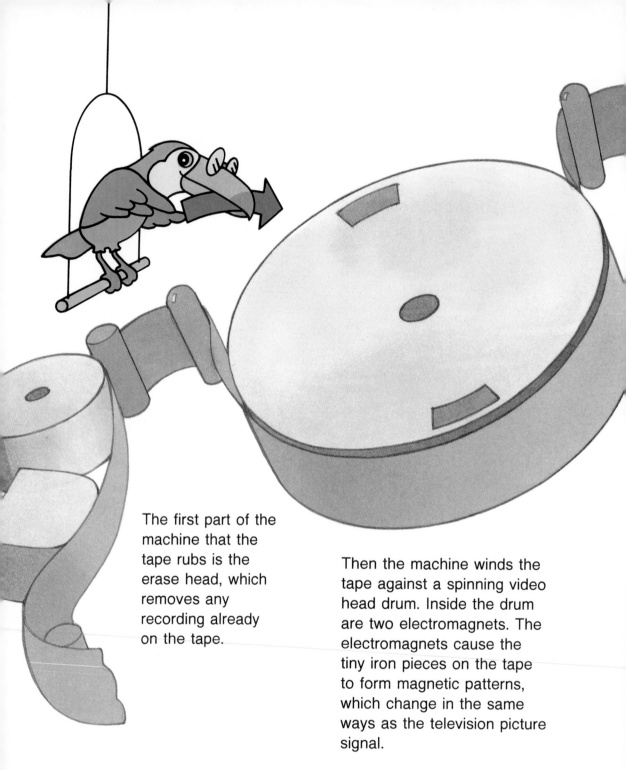

The first part of the machine that the tape rubs is the erase head, which removes any recording already on the tape.

Then the machine winds the tape against a spinning video head drum. Inside the drum are two electromagnets. The electromagnets cause the tiny iron pieces on the tape to form magnetic patterns, which change in the same ways as the television picture signal.

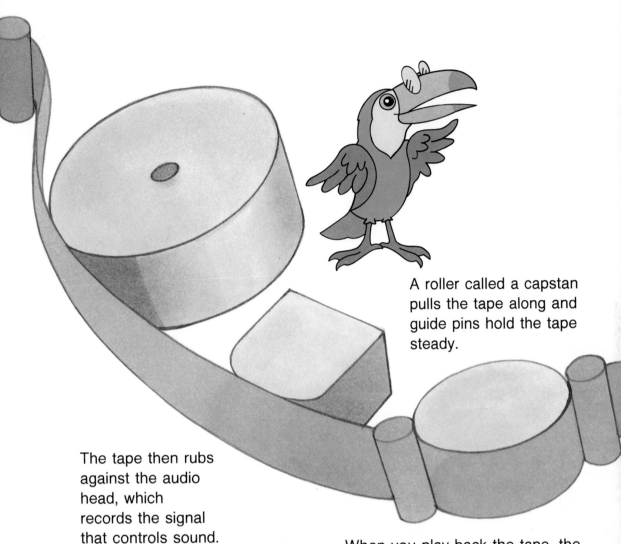

A roller called a capstan pulls the tape along and guide pins hold the tape steady.

The tape then rubs against the audio head, which records the signal that controls sound. The tape moves smoothly past the video and audio heads, recording as it goes.

When you play back the tape, the magnetic patterns on the tape cause electric currents to flow in the heads. These currents go to the television, which uses them as if they were signals broadcast from a TV studio.

But the "studio" was right in the VCR. Meanwhile, you, the engineer, were out playing baseball or whatever, while the studio was doing all the work!

The producer is team captain. The producer comes up with the idea for the program and assembles the people who will bring off the show.

Getting the Show on the Air

Putting on a television show is a team effort. Come meet some of the players:

The director turns the producer's idea into pictures by guiding the actors and the crew.

The production assistant hands out the scripts to the actors, keeps track of props, and arranges for meals on the set, among other duties.

The writer comes up with the actors' words and stage directions.

The audio, or sound, engineer records and sometimes creates the sounds, such as explosions, for a show.

The lighting director decides what lights to use for different effects.

ON THE AIR

The makeup artist helps the actors with their faces and hair so that they look right for their parts.

The art director plans the sets, which are all the things you see in the background for a show. He or she is in charge of getting the sets built for the show.

The camera operator tapes what the director asks for.

The costume designer chooses the clothes the actors will wear.

213

Did You Know?

Props include everything from the furniture in the room to a fork on the table. Many times props only look like the real thing. Some objects that appear heavy on television, such as lampposts, are made of lightweight balsa wood. Even small objects may be fakes. For example, if a script calls for an actor to break a vase, the vase may be made of sugar, melted and made to look like glass.

The Lights, Camera, Action Game

The object of the game on the next two pages is to reach the last space—"ON THE AIR" as quickly as possible. Use a button or a colored square of paper as a marker. Before each move, toss two pennies as if they were dice. If both pennies land heads up, you may move three spaces. If both pennies land tails up, you may move two spaces. If one penny lands heads up and another lands tails up, move one space. Begin on the space marked "START!" Play a few rounds and compare your speeds.

More good news:
The ideal co-star
is found.

OUT TO LUNCH

DIRECTOR

Fetch!

Good news:
A big-name star is
interested *and* the
money for the show
comes through!

The director is busy
on another show.
Wait 30 seconds.

The writer whips
out a script in
record time.

The producer cannot
find money to put on
the show. Go back
to START.

The producer gets
an idea for a show.

START!

34   1

The production assistant loses important props. Wait 30 seconds.

Authentic costumes are unavailable, so the costume designer makes do.

The star spends 3 hours with the makeup artist. Go back a space.

The camera operator plans his shots during rehearsal. The lighting director adjusts the spotlights. Wait 10 seconds.

CRASH!

The art director halts production. Wait 2 minutes while she redoes the scenery.

The audio engineer searches the sound effects library for the right tape. Go back 3 spaces while he looks.

LION ROAR

ON THE AIR

Pennies, an

Dimes, d Dollar$

THINGS WE SAVE AND SPEND

Who draws the pictures on dollar bills?

Where are pennies made?

How does the cash register "know" what you bought?

How Money Came About

Just think if money grew on trees! You could have your own money tree and the money would just grow whenever you needed it. Oh well . . . too bad. Money never has grown on trees, but it does have an unusual history.

People used to trade, or "barter," for the things they wanted before we had money. Certain goods—salt, cattle, gold objects, for example—were always welcome for trade. In time, people began to use the popular trade items as money. Long ago in a land called ancient Egypt, something might have been worth ten cattle, or twenty cattle. The cattle might be used to "buy" different things.

What other kinds of money have people used? That depends on what was valuable to them, and how they could organize a supply of this important thing called money.

Some American Indian tribes used shell money called wampum. The Indians collected shells of different shades and made them into beads. After polishing the beads, the Indians strung them into belts and necklaces. The wampum was used to trade for other items.

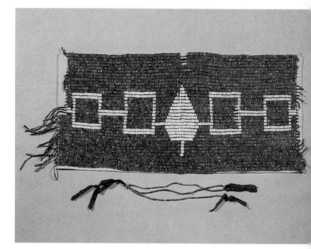

The Quetzal (keht SAHL) bird is rare and is found only from southern Mexico to Panama. Indians called Aztecs used the tail feathers from these brightly colored birds as a form of money.

One of the most unusual forms of money was used on the Yap Islands in the South Pacific Ocean. Here the islanders used large, wheel-shaped "coins" made of limestone. The coins ranged in size: The larger the stone, the more valuable it was. Islanders carried the large coins on a pole passed through a hole in the center of the coin.

True coins were made in an Asian kingdom called Lydia about 2,700 years ago. The coins were a blend of gold and silver. In time, they became all the same size and weight. "How convenient," merchants and traders must have thought. The idea caught on.

According to legend, a Chinese emperor first used money similar to paper money about 2,200 years ago. As the story goes, the emperor had the hide of a prized white stag cut into small pieces. Then he made each piece worth 40,000 bronze coins. When visitors came to honor the emperor, he sold these "White Stag notes" for cash.

The examples go on and on. Wherever money comes from or how it has been made, though, one thing hasn't changed much: We still like to have it, save it, and spend it!

Making Money

The first coins made at the United States Mint in Philadelphia were probably made from President George Washington's melted silver tea sets and candlesticks.

Coins are still made, or minted, in Philadelphia. And some special coins contain silver. But the coins we use every day have no silver. They're made of alloys, which are mixtures of metals. Pennies are mostly zinc with a copper coating. Dimes, quarters, half dollars, and dollars are metal-layer sandwiches. The center is copper, and the outer layers are a mixture of copper and nickel.

Copper

Copper and nickel

How does the Mint make a coin? Let's start with the design that you see on both sides. An artist created the design and the government approved it. The artist then carved the design on a large coin model.

How was the design then made to fit the small coin? A machine carves a coin-sized version of the design into a "hub," which is a softened piece of steel.

Next this "master hub" is hardened and used to make steel stamps called "master dies." These dies make copies of the master hub, which, in turn, produce the dies that stamp out millions of coins each year.

Before coins can be stamped, the metal alloys must be prepared. Metals are melted and poured into molds. The alloys come out in bars. Penny and nickel bars are rolled into strips, much like a pie crust is rolled with a rolling pin.

Bars for dimes, quarters, half dollars, and dollars are made from three layers of metal. These thin layers are rolled out separately. Then they are pressed together and rolled to the right thickness.

A machine punches out blank coins from the strips of metal. These blanks are heated slightly. This softens the coins, making them easier to stamp with the design. Afterward, they are washed and tumble-dried to make the coins shiny.

Next, the blanks move through a machine that forms that slightly raised edge on each coin. See if you can feel this edge on some of your coins. A screening machine then tests the blanks to make sure they're perfectly shaped.

Next, it's time for the coining press. In this machine, two steel dies hit the blank at the same time, pressing the designs into the coin.

Finally, it's off to banks for these shiny new coins. From there, they will jingle their way into pockets, piggy banks, stores, and, well, just about everywhere!

Dollar Dozen Game

You Will Need:

empty egg carton
10 pennies
8 nickels
4 quarters
scratch paper
pencil

Here's a brainteaser for you. See if you can make just 12 of these 22 coins add up to 100 cents, or a dollar.

1. Sort the coins into three piles: pennies, nickels, and quarters.

2. Use your paper and pencil to try to come up with a combination of 12 coins that would add up to 100 cents.

3. Use the egg carton to help in the adding, too. As you figure, place one coin in each little cup. You solved the brainteaser if you fill all 12 cups and the coins add up to a dollar.

Variation: Start with these coins and see if you can get 12 of them to add up to a dollar: 3 quarters, 15 nickels.

Answers on page 243

*Don't forget to ask your parents for permission.

Paper Bills

Imagine having to pay for everything you buy with coins. If you wanted to buy something, a new bike or something else expensive, you might have to use hundreds or thousands of coins to pay for it. You probably could not even carry all the coins by yourself!

As you can see, using paper money is much more convenient than using coins alone. Paper currency, which is another term for money, in the United States is made by the Bureau of Engraving and Printing, a branch of our government's Treasury.

Feel a crisp dollar bill. Does it seem different from a piece of regular paper? That's because money is printed on a special paper made from linen and cotton fibers, not wood fibers. If you look closely, too, you will notice tiny red and blue silk threads running through the paper. These threads make money more difficult to copy, or counterfeit (**KOWN** turh fiht).

Just as with coin minting, making paper money begins with a sketch of the design for the bill. The sketch is engraved onto a soft steel plate.

A machine called a transfer press next transfers the design onto a soft steel roller. The roller is hardened and then used to engrave 32 copies of the bill onto a steel plate. Separate plates print the front and back of bills.

The ink used to print money is made from a secret formula. To guard the formula, all leftover ink is collected at the end of a day of printing.

Next, high-speed presses print the paper currency on the special paper. The press can print 8,000 sheets of bills each hour.

Afterward, machines cut, count, wrap, and band the bills.

After more sorting and piling, the currency is stored or shipped to banks run by the government. From there, the bills will travel all over the world. And some of them will end up as a gift or allowance to you.

Money That Makes Money

"Wow! Twenty dollars!" exclaimed
Alice, opening her birthday card.
"Thanks a lot, Aunt Kate!" she
said, giving her aunt a hug.

"What do you think you'll do
with the money?" asked Kate.

"I suppose I'll put it in my
piggy bank. I'm hoping to save
money for a bike. This money will
help," answered Alice.

"Well, it's good to save your money," Kate noted, "but why don't you put it in an account at a savings bank or a savings and loan?"

"What difference does it make?" asked Alice, "I'm still saving my money either way—right?"

"That's true, but in a savings account, your money earns money for you," Kate explained. "You see," she went on, "banks don't just keep your money, they use it to make more money. They give it to other people as loans. The bank charges a fee for the loan. It's called interest. Then the bank pays you for letting it use your money. That money you earn is also called interest."

233

Alice watched Kate write some figures on a piece of paper.

"Let's say you earn five cents for every dollar you have in your account each year," Kate began. "With twenty dollars, you'll earn an extra dollar, making your total savings twenty-one dollars.

"That extra dollar may not seem like too much, but it adds up if you have more and more money in the account. Think how much interest you'd earn on 500 dollars."

Alice bit on the end of her pencil, then did some figures.

"Wow!" cried Alice. "I'd earn *twenty-five* more dollars in interest!"

"So, are you still going to put your money in your piggy bank?" asked Kate.

Smiling at her aunt, Alice answered, "I think I like this way of getting money. Thanks for the birthday present, Aunt Kate—and the tip."

Make a Money Saver

You Will Need:

cardboard ice cream
    or yogurt container
    with a snug lid, 1
    pint size
light-colored
    construction paper
colored pencils or
    crayons
1 penny
1 nickel
1 quarter
1 dime
scissors
glue or tape

1. Measure and cut your construction paper to fit around the container.

2. Trace the top of the container and cut.

3. Make coin rubbings on your papers. Place a coin under the paper and rub your colored pencil or crayon over the coin. You will see the coin's design come through. Repeat with different coins until you have enough for a nice design.

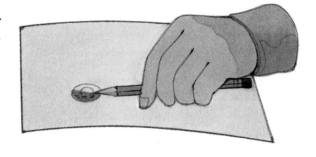

4. Glue or tape your papers around the container and on the top.

5. Cut a hole in the top of the container big enough to let coins slip through.

Use your new bank to save your money.

*Don't forget to ask your parents for permission.

Check It Out

Let's say your family wants to buy something expensive. How about a computer or a purebred puppy? Your parents might not carry enough money around to pay in cash for the purchase. The cash could get lost or stolen. Perhaps they will use a check instead. Checks are like order blanks for cash. They say "please pay _____ this much money: _____."

When your parents receive money for working, they might put some of it into a checking account at a bank or savings and loan association. The bank holds the money and gives out checks, which your parents write out to buy things.

What happens to the check—for the computer, for example? The store owner brings it to his or her own bank. That bank will give the owner the purchase price or will put that amount into the store's account. Banks work together to help people use checks.

Make up some fun checks next time
you play "store" or "shopping." But
you'll have to wait until you grow up to
write out real checks!

How Does the Price Get into the Cash Register?

When you go to the grocery store, look at a cereal box, a can of soup, or another packaged product. Do you see the little square of dark and light lines printed on the package? This symbol is called a bar code. Bar codes are a computerized way to speed pricing and checkout of the things we buy in stores.

The dark and light spaces in the code tell the name of the product, the package size, the manufacturer, and, sometimes, the price. Who can read these special codes? A machine called an optical (AHP tih kuhl) scanner. Optical scanners produce beams of bright light that "see" the code and translate what it means.

At the grocery store, the clerk usually slides the bar code over a small window built into the counter. The scanner is under this window and sends a beam of light rays across the code. Light reflects off the light-colored spaces only, producing a series of light and dark pulses. A detector picks up these pulses and changes them into electrical signals.

The electrical signals travel to a store computer. The computer makes the price appear on the cash register and adds up the bill. The product name and price then appear on the register tape.

Speed, light rays, special codes, and computers just to organize the way we buy things today? We've come a long way from the days of trading for the things we needed, with no money!

Stores Go Shopping

How would you like the job of choosing the different toys or sneakers that we buy in a store? It sounds like fun, doesn't it? Well, it really is a job. Someone has to *get* the things that we will spend our money on in stores. People who do this are called buyers.

Buyers must try to figure out what people will like. They usually have to predict what shoppers will buy a few months or even a year into the future.

Buyers visit factory showrooms, where samples of different items, such as sneakers, are on display. A buyer thinks, "Next spring, will kids want purple sneakers, striped sneakers, or polka-dotted ones?" That buyer will probably order all three styles and more!

Clothing buyers may attend fashion shows. They watch models who wear new styles of clothing.

The buyers must decide
which styles their
customers will like most,
and which styles will sell
best in their store.

Another place where
buyers can shop is at a
trade show. (When used
this way, *trade* means
business or industry.)
Buyers come to trade
shows from all over the
world. There are
housewares shows, toy
shows, electronics shows,
and more.

Can you imagine a toy
trade show? Most are so

big that it takes more than one day just to see everything. Wonderful toys are on display everywhere. It's fascinating and fun, but for buyers it's also hard work!

answers: dollar dozen game

3 quarters, 4 nickels, and 5 pennies add up to one dollar; 10 nickels and 2 quarters also add up to one dollar.

Books to Read

Books can help us discover more about where things come from and how they work. Your school or public library may have the books in this list, as well as others.

Ages 5-8

Bits and Bytes by Seymour Simon (Crowell, 1985)

If you think all bugs crawl and boots are only to be worn, then it's time to discover the special language of computers. EZ the robot makes everything fun to learn.

How Is a Crayon Made? by Oz Charles (Simon and Schuster, 1988)

Take a trip through a crayon factory and see beautiful, close-up photos of crayons being made. Also by the same author: *How Does Soda Get into a Bottle?*

If You Made a Million by David M. Schwartz (Lothrop, Lee & Shepard, 1989)

A magician named Marvelosissimo helps you explore ways to earn and save money. You might even have enough to pay for a castle or a ticket to the moon!

Night Markets Bringing Food to a City by Joshua Horwitz (Crowell, 1984)

While most people are sleeping, workers are busy delivering supplies to stores and markets. Clear photographs make readers feel they are right on the scene.

Picking & Weaving by Bijou LeTord (Four Winds Press, 1980)

This is the story of cotton, from the fields to the textile mill and then to the store, where people buy yards of fabric. The author's bright pictures and designs are a treat.

The Magic School Bus at the Waterworks by Joanna Cole (Scholastic, 1986)

Join Ms. Frizzle's class as they learn about water in a truly remarkable way. Follow the path that water takes from a mountain stream to the place you live.

Ages 9-12

Bat, Ball, Glove by William Jaspersohn (Little, Brown, 1989)

If you enjoy the game of baseball, you will like finding out how logs become bats and leather becomes gloves. Photographs also show how uniforms are made and all the steps in making baseballs.

The Big Stretch: The Complete Book of the Amazing Rubber Band by Ada and Frank Graham (Knopf, 1985)

How did the invention of the rubber band change people's lives? Read some fascinating facts about rubber bands and learn how to use them in creative ways.

Computer Sense, Computer Nonsense by Seymour Simon (Lippincott, 1984)

Do computers work better on rainy days? This book answers that question and gives useful advice about what to believe and not believe about computers.

First Class! The Postal System in Action by Harold Roth (Pantheon, 1983)

See what happens to letters and packages as they travel to their destination. You will appreciate how postal workers keep things running smoothly.

From Hand to Mouth: Or, How We Invented Knives, Forks, Spoons, & Chopsticks & The Table Manners to Go With Them by James Giblin (Crowell, 1987)

Can you guess which came first—the knife, fork, or spoon? Many interesting facts are presented in this humorous history of eating habits around the world.

How a Book Is Made by Aliki (Crowell, 1986)

In cartoon style, the author's pictures show the stages of bookmaking—from idea to bound book. Thought balloons and labels make the whole process fun and easy to understand.

The Secret Life of School Supplies by Vicki Cobb (Lippincott, 1981)

Pencils, paper, chalk, and other everyday supplies have a history all their own. Do you want to try making some items yourself? Some easy directions are included.

Sneakers Meet Your Feet by Vicki Cobb (Little, Brown, 1985)

Some facts about your amazing feet may surprise you. Then see how cloth, rubber, and leather are put together in a sneaker factory.

The Way Things Work by David Macaulay (Doubleday, 1988)

From air conditioners to zoom lenses, find out how hundreds of things work—as well as some fascinating connections, such as how a dentist's drill is related to a windmill.

New Words

Here are some words you have met in this book. Many of them may be new to you. All are useful words to know. Next to each word, you'll see how to say the word: **abacus** (AB uh kuhs). The part in capital letters is said more loudly than the rest of the word. One or two sentences tell the word's meaning as it is used in this book.

abacus (AB uh kuhs) An abacus is an ancient tool used for mathematical problems. It is a frame with wires or rods on which beads move up and down.

animation (an ih MAY shuhn) Animation is a way of making and photographing pictures to make them look as if they are moving.

artificial (ahr tuh FISH uhl) Artificial means made by people and not found in nature. Vanillin is an artificial vanilla flavor.

bacteria (bak TIH ree uh) Bacteria are very tiny plants that can only be seen through a microscope. Most bacteria are harmless, but some can cause disease.

barter (BAHR tuhr) Barter is a system of trading one thing for another rather than using money.

bearing (BAIR ihng) In a wheel, a bearing is one of several small balls that roll smoothly and keep the wheel parts from scraping against each other.

buyer (BYE uhr) A buyer is the person who chooses and purchases the items a store will sell.

cacao (kuh KAY oh) A cacao is an evergreen tree found in tropical regions. Its seeds are used to make chocolate and cocoa.

calculator (KAL kyoo lay tuhr) A calculator is a machine that is designed to solve math problems.

cel (SEHL) A cel is a sheet of clear plastic on which each individual drawing of a cartoon is made.

cellulose (SEHL yuh lohs) Cellulose is a fiber found in trees, grass, and other plants. It is used in making paper and other products.

checking account (CHEHK ihng ah KOWNT) A checking account is the funds a customer keeps in the bank from which to write checks, or payment orders.

chemical (KEM uh kuhl) A chemical is any one of the many substances that make up our world and the things we use. Chemicals can be found in nature (oxygen in air), or they can be produced in laboratories for use in making things such as medicines and plastics.

circuit (SUR kuht) In a computer, a circuit is a complete path upon which electronic signals travel.

combine (KAHM byn) A combine is a farm machine used to cut wheat and other crops and separate seeds from stalks.

computer (kuhm PYOO tur) A computer is an electronic machine that stores, calculates, and helps process information at high speed.

computer chip (kuhm PYOO tur CHIHP) A computer chip is a small wafer of the chemical silicon containing electrical pathways and switches that carry a computer's electrical signals and commands.

concentrated (KAHN sehn trayt ehd) Concentrated juice is strong and thick with little or no water added.

currency (KUH rehn cee) Currency is another word for money.

detergent (dih TUR jehnt) Detergent is a synthetic product used for cleaning. It is like soap in many ways, but made from different ingredients.

diaphragm (DY uh fram) In a telephone, a diaphragm is a thin metal disk in both the receiving and transmitting parts of the handset. The diaphragms vibrate when sound waves reach them and they send a flow of electricity to help both to receive and transmit the phone caller's voice.

electromagnet (ih lek troh MAG neht) In a telephone, an electromagnet is the part of the phone's receiver that becomes a magnet when electric current flows through it. The electromagnet then makes sound waves that go on to create the sound of a voice on the phone.

enzyme (EHN zym) An enzyme is a certain kind of chemical. It helps to cause a change in other substances, such as when the enzyme rennin causes milk to thicken while cheese is being made.

fiber (FYE bur) A fiber is a very thin thread of a material such as wool, cotton, or cellulose.

gear (GEAHR) A gear is a wheel with teeth on its edges. The teeth fit into another gear or a chain to make a rotating motion that drives a bicycle or other machine.

interest (IHN trest) As a money term, interest is the earnings that a bank pays its customers when they have an account in the bank. Interest also is the fee charged to people who borrow money from the bank.

manuscript (MAN yoo skript) A manuscript is the typed copy of a book that will be printed.

mineral (MIHN ur uhl) A mineral is one of the thousands of nonliving substances found in nature. Salt and gold are examples of minerals.

money (MUN ee) Money is whatever people have used to buy things or services with. Today money is almost always in the form of coins, paper bills, and checks.

optical scanner (AHP tih kuhl SKAN nur) An optical scanner is a machine that produces bright lights that can see and translate a bar code on a package being bought.

paraffin (PAR uh fihn) Paraffin is a wax used in making crayons and candles.

pasteurization (pas chuhr uh ZAY shuhn) Pasteurization is a heating process used to kill harmful germs in milk and other foods.

pigment (PIHG mehnt) A pigment is a powder used to give color to something, such as crayons or paint.

plastics (PLAS tikz) Plastics are synthetic materials made from chemicals. They can be shaped into many forms.

pulp (PUHLP) Pulp is the watery mixture that is made when wood chips are boiled.

react (ree ACT) With chemicals, react means to change. One chemical can cause another substance to change and take a new form.

receiver (rih CEE vuhr) A receiver is the part of a phone that you listen to in order to hear a caller's voice.

reservoir (REHZ ur vwar) A reservoir is a place that stores water for people to use. Reservoirs can be natural (lakes) or they can be made for the purpose.

resin (REHZ uhn) A resin is the basic form of plastic before it is made into a plastic object such as a toy or cup. Natural resins from trees are sticky liquids that can be used in paint to make the paint dry.

rivet (RIHV iht) A rivet is a metal bolt used to fasten things together strongly.

satellite (SAT uh lyte) A satellite that carries television or telephone signals long distances is a spacecraft that orbits the earth with equipment for transmitting the signals for broadcast.

sewage (SOO ihj) Sewage is the wastewater that flows from houses and other places to a treatment plant to be cleaned and purified.

scale (SKAYL) Scale is the size of a model compared with the size the model represents.

signal (SIHG nuhl) In communications, a signal is the pattern of sound or picture that is carried through the air for a telephone, radio, and television connection.

solution (sah LOO shuhn) A solution is a liquid mixture made by dissolving one or more ingredients, such as salt, into water or another liquid.

sound waves (SOWND WAYVES) Sound waves are the vibrations caused by voices, music, or anything that produces noise. Sound waves travel through the air.

superimposing (soo per im POZE ihng) Superimposing is the putting of one thing on top of another. Two pieces of film can be superimposed to show a person against a sky background, for example.

synthetic (sihn THET ik) Synthetic means made by people and not found in nature. Nylon is a synthetic fabric. Wool is a natural fabric.

trade (TRAYD) In business, trade means having to do with one kind of product or industry. For example, buyers from the clothing *trade* get together to choose new styles for their store.

transmit (trans MIHT) Transmit means to send. When you speak into a phone's mouthpiece, your words are transmitted to the listener.

transmitter (tranz MIH tur) A transmitter is the part of a telephone's mouthpiece into which you speak; it sends the signal made by the sound of your voice to the listener.

videocassette recorder (VIH dee oh kuhs seht ree KAWR dur) A videocassette recorder (VCR) is a machine that can put pictures and sound, as from a television show, on magnetic tape and then play them back so you can watch a show at a later time.

yeast (YEEST) Yeast is an ingredient used in baking to make dough rise. It is made of tiny fungus plant cells.

ZIP Code (ZIHP COHD) A ZIP Code is a number that stands for a state, city, and neighborhood in the United States. The ZIP Code system speeds up mail delivery.

Illustration Acknowledgments

The publishers of *Childcraft* gratefully acknowledge the courtesy of the following photographers, agencies, and organizations for illustrations in this volume. When all the illustrations for a sequence of pages are from a single source, the inclusive page numbers are given. Credits should be read from left to right, top to bottom, on their respective pages. All illustrations are the exclusive property of the publishers of *Childcraft* unless names are marked with an asterisk (*).

Cover: Aristocrat, Discovery, and Standard
Bindings—Roberta Polfus
Heritage Binding—Eldon Doty; Eileen Mueller
Neill; Robert Byrd; Eldon Doty; Eileen Mueller
Neill; Roberta Polfus; Eileen Mueller Neill
1–3: Donna Kae Nelson
4–7: Robert Byrd
8–9: Joe Rogers
10–11: Donna Kae Nelson
12–13: Robert Byrd
14–15: Robert Byrd; Joe Rogers
16–17: Robert Byrd
18–19: Ethel Gold
20–21: Joe Rogers; Eldon Doty
22–23: Larry LeFever, Grant Heilman*; Eldon Doty
24–25: Ethel Gold; Lane Yerkes; Joe Rogers
26–27: Lane Yerkes; © Charles Gupton, The Stock
Market*
28–29: Robert Byrd
30–31: Lynn L. Bell; Joe Rogers
32–33: Lynn L. Bell; Joe Rogers
34–35: Lane Yerkes; David R. Frazier; Joe Rogers
36–37: Eldon Doty
38–39: Lane Yerkes; Joe Rogers; McCormick/Schilling
Spices*
40–41: Lane Yerkes; McCormick/Schilling Spices*; Lane
Yerkes
42–43: Joe Rogers; Eldon Doty
44–45: Eldon Doty; Ethel Gold; Joe Rogers
46–49: Larry Frederick
50–51: Donna Kae Nelson
52–57: Eileen Mueller Neill
58–59: Conner Prairie*; Joe Rogers; Eldon Doty
60–61: Susan Schmidt; Lever Brothers Company*
62–63: Ethel Gold; Eldon Doty; Joe Rogers
64–65: Eldon Doty; Comfort Manufacturing Company
(Ralph Brunke); Steven Spicer
66–67: Richard Loehle; Steven Spicer
68–69: John O. Butler Co.*; Len Ebert; Lydia Halverson
70–71: Lydia Halverson; Joe Rogers
72–73: Donna Kae Nelson
74–75: David R. Frazier
76–77: Robert Byrd; Larry LeFever, Grant Heilman*;
Burlington Industries, Inc.*
78–79: John Holder; © Peter Gonzalez*
80–81: Len Ebert
82–83: John Holder; Robert Byrd
84–85: Artstreet*; J. P. Stevens & Co.*; © Seth Goltzer, The
Stock Market*; Robert Byrd
86–87: Len Ebert; David R. Frazier; John Holder
88–89: Eldon Doty; Joe Rogers; David R. Frazier
90–91: Steven Spicer; Joe Rogers; SPL from Photo
Researchers*; © Michael Abbey, Photo
Researchers*; Robert Byrd
92–93: Eldon Doty; Joe Rogers
94–95: John Holder
96–97: Eldon Doty; Converse *
98–99: Donna Kae Nelson
100–101: Nan Brooks; Binney & Smith Inc.*
102–103: Binney & Smith Inc.*; Nan Brooks; Binney & Smith
Inc.*; Len Ebert
104–105: Steven Spicer
106–107: Len Ebert; Rawlings Sporting Goods Co.*; Joe
Rogers
108–109: Eileen Mueller Neill; Joe Rogers
110–111: The Granger Collection*; Lydia Halverson
112–113: Lydia Halverson; Len Ebert
114–115: Jared D. Lee
116–117: David R. Frazier; Jared D. Lee; David R. Frazier
118–119: Jared D. Lee; David R. Frazier

120–121: Lydia Halverson
122–123: Lydia Halverson; Joe Rogers
124–125: Chevrolet Motor Division, General Motors Corp.*;
Steven Spicer; Eileen Mueller Neill
126–127: Eileen Mueller Neill; David R. Frazier; Artstreet*;
David R. Frazier
128–129: Joe Rogers; © J. T. Miller, The Stock Market*
130–131: Eileen Mueller Neill; Len Ebert
132–133: Eileen Mueller Neill; Steven Spicer
134–135: Eileen Mueller Neill
136–137: © Hank Morgan, SPL from Photo Researchers*;
Eileen Mueller Neill
138–139: Donna Kae Nelson
140–141: Eileen Mueller Neill; Joe Rogers
142–143: Len Ebert; Eileen Mueller Neill; Jan Palmer
144–145: David R. Frazier
146–147: Brenda Tropinski; Steven Spicer; Brian Karas;
James River Corp.*
148–149: Brian Karas; James River Corp.*
150–151: Len Ebert
152–153: Jared D. Lee; Joe Rogers
154–155: Jared D. Lee; Joe Rogers
156–157: Jared D. Lee
158–159: Jan Palmer
160–161: David R. Frazier
162–163: Brian Karas
164–165: Joe Rogers; IBM*
166–167: Donna Kae Nelson
168–169: Richard Loehle; AT&T Bell Laboratories*; Steven
Spicer
170–171: Eileen Mueller Neill; © David R. Frazier
Photolibrary*
172–173: Eileen Mueller Neill
174–175: Eileen Mueller Neill; Porta-Tel*
176–177: Eileen Mueller Neill; GTE*; Steven Spicer
178–179: Steven Spicer; Richard Loehle; The Granger
Collection*; Robert A. Siegel, Inc.*
180–181: Bureau of Engraving and Printing*; © David R.
Frazier Photolibrary*
182–183: © David R. Frazier Photolibrary*; Len Ebert; Ethel
Gold
184–185: Lydia Halverson; Joe Rogers
186–187: © Cameron Davidson, Bruce Coleman, Inc.*;
Steven Spicer; © David R. Frazier Photolibrary*; ©
Cameron Davidson, Bruce Coleman, Inc.*; Lydia
Halverson
188–189: Ethel Gold
190–191: Donna Kae Nelson
192–193: Jared D. Lee; Joe Rogers
194–195: Reprinted by permission of UFS, Inc.*; Jared D.
Lee
196–197: Len Ebert; Copyright © by Universal Pictures, a
Division of Universal City Studios, Inc. Courtesy of
MCA Publishing Rights, a Division of MCA Inc.*
198–199: © Lucasfilm Ltd. All rights reserved.*
200–201: Robert Byrd; *Planet of the Apes* ©, Apjac
Productions, Inc. and 20th Century Fox Film
Corporation. All rights reserved.*
202–203: © Lucasfilm Ltd. All rights reserved.*
204–207: Eileen Mueller Neill
208–209: Joe Rogers; Len Ebert
210–211: Joe Rogers; Len Ebert
212–213: Eldon Doty
214–215: Copyright © Walt Disney Company*; Eldon Doty
216–217: Eldon Doty
218–219: Donna Kae Nelson
220–221: Robert Byrd; New York State Museum, State
Education Department*
222–223: Lane Yerkes; Smithsonian Institution, National
Numismatic Collection*
224–225: Susan Schmidt; *Childcraft* photo
226–227: *Childcraft* photo; Susan Schmidt
228–229: Len Ebert; Susan Schmidt
230–231: Joe Rogers; *Childcraft* photo
232–233: Eileen Mueller Neill
234–235: Eileen Mueller Neill; Len Ebert
236–237: Lane Yerkes
238–239: Cameramann International, Ltd.*; Bob Byrd
240–241: © Chuck O'Rear, West Light*; Eldon Doty
242–243: Eldon Doty; Joe Rogers

Index

This index is an alphabetical list of the important topics covered in this book. It will help you find information given in both words *and* pictures. To help you understand what an entry means, there is sometimes a helping word in parentheses. For example, *alloy* (metal). If there is information in both words and pictures, you will see the words *with pictures* after the page number. If there is *only* a picture, you will see the word *picture* before the page number.

World Book Encyclopedia, Inc. provides high quality educational and reference products for the family and school, including a FIVE-VOLUME CHILDCRAFT FAVORITES SET, colorful books on favorite topics, such as DOGS and INDIANS; and THE WORLD BOOK MEDICAL ENCYCLOPEDIA, a 1,040-page, fully illustrated family health reference. For further information, write WORLD BOOK ENCYCLOPEDIA, INC., P.O. Box 3073, Evanston, IL 60204.